Taurus

21 April – 21 May

First published in Great Britain 2009
by Harlequin Mills & Boon Limited,
Eton House, 18-24 Paradise Road, Richmond, Surrey TW9 1SR

Copyright © Dadhichi Toth 2008 & 2009

ISBN: 978 0 263 87065 7

Typeset at Midland Typesetters Australia

Harlequin Mills & Boon policy is to use papers that are natural, renewable and recyclable products and made from wood grown in sustainable forests. The logging and manufacturing processes conform to the legal environmental regulations of the country of origin.

Printed and bound in Spain
by Litografia Rosés S.A., Barcelona

About
Dadhichi

Dadhichi is one of Australia's foremost astrologers. He has the ability to draw from complex astrological theory to provide clear, easily understandable advice and insights for people who want to know what their future might hold.

In the 26 years that Dadhichi has been practising astrology, face reading and other esoteric studies, he has conducted over 9,500 consultations. His clients include celebrities, political and diplomatic figures, and media and corporate identities from all over the world.

Dadhichi's unique blend of astrology and face reading helps people fulfil their true potential. His extensive experience practising western astrology is complemented by his research into the theory and practice of eastern systems of astrology.

Dadhichi features in numerous newspapers and magazines and he also appears regularly on many of Australia's leading television and radio networks, where many of his political and worldwide forecasts have proved uncannily accurate.

His website www.astrology.com.au is now one of the top ten online Australian lifestyle sites and, in conjunction with www.facereader.com, www.soulconnector.com and www.psychjuice.com, they attract over half a million visitors monthly. The websites offer a wide variety of features, helpful information and personal services.

Dedicated to The Light of Intuition
Sri V. Krishnaswamy — mentor and friend
With thanks to Julie, Joram, Isaac and Janelle

Welcome from
Dadhichi

Dear Friend,

Welcome! It's great to have you here, reading your horoscope, trying to learn more about yourself and what's in store for you in 2010.

I visited Mexico a while ago and stumbled upon the Mayan prophecies for 2012, which, they say, is the year when the longstanding calendar we use in the western world supposedly stops! If taken literally, some people could indeed believe that 'the end of the world is near'. However, I see it differently.

Yes, it might seem as though the world is getting harder and harder to deal with, especially when fear enters our lives. But, I believe that 'the end' indicated by these Mayan prophecies has more to do with the end that will create new beginnings for our societies, more to do with making changes to our material view of life and some necessary adjustments for the human race to progress and prosper in future. So let's get one thing straight: you and I will both be around after 2012, reading our 2013 horoscopes!

My prediction and advice centres around keeping a cool mind and not reacting to the fear that could overtake us. Of course, this isn't easy, especially when media messages might increase our anxiety about such things as the impacts of global warming or the scarcity of fossil fuels.

I want you to understand that it is certainly important to be aware and play your part in making the world a better place; however, the best and surest way to support global goals is to help yourself first. Let me explain. If everyone focused just a little more on improving *themselves* rather than just pointing their finger to criticise others, it would result in a dramatic change and improvement; not just globally, but societally. And, of course, you mustn't forget what a positive impact this would have on your personal relationships as well.

Astrology focuses on self-awareness; your own insights into your personality, thinking processes and relationships. This is why this small book you have in your hand doesn't only concentrate on what is going to happen, but more importantly how you can *make* things happen positively through being your best.

I have always said that there are two types of people: puppets and actors. The first simply react to each outside stimulus and are therefore slaves of their environment, and even of their own minds and emotions. They are puppets in the hands of karma. The other group I call actors. Although they can't control what happens to them all the time, either, they are better able to adapt and gain something purposeful in their lives. They are in no way victims of circumstance.

I hope you will use what is said in the following pages to become the master of your destiny, and not rely on the predictions that are given as mere fate but as valuable guidelines to use intelligently when life presents you with its certain challenges.

Neither the outside world, nor the ups and downs that occur in your life, should affect your innermost spirituality and self-confidence. Take control: look beyond your current challenges and use them as the building blocks of experience to create success and fulfilment in the coming year.

I believe you have the power to become great and shine your light for all to see. I hope your 2010 horoscope book will be a helpful guide and inspiration for you.

Warm regards, and may the stars shine brightly for you in 2010!

Your Astrologer,

Dadhichi Toth

Contents

The Taurus
Identity

The laws of science do not distinguish between the past and the future.

—Steven W. Hawking

Taurus: A Snapshot

Key Characteristics

Security conscious, determined, sensual, loyal, steady, proud, obstinate and decisive

Compatible Star Signs

Virgo, Capricorn and Pisces

Key Life Phrase

I have

Life Goals

To feel secure and settled; to have a rich and comfortable life

Platinum Assets

Determination, steadiness and loyalty

Zodiac Totem

The Bull

Zodiac Symbol

Zodiac Facts

Second sign of the zodiac; fixed, fruitful, feminine and moist

Element

Earth

Famous Taureans

Barbra Streisand, Uma Thurman, Cher, Billy Joel, Grace Jones, The Reverend Jim Jones, Jessica Lange, Jay Leno, Renee Zellweger, Kirsten Dunst, George Clooney, Queen Elizabeth II, Jack Nicholson, Janet Jackson

Taurus: Your profile

'Salt of the earth' is how most people would describe you, Taurus. There's something very settling about the energies your star sign endows you with. Steady, enduring, reliable and extremely loyal are some of the typical descriptions that come to mind when I try to sum up your character.

Those who are closest to you wouldn't disagree with what I have to say; but then, they also know the other side of you, too, don't they? Descriptions like stubborn, pig-headed or opinionated probably sound familiar to you, right? I think the more gracious way of describing you is strong-minded, persistent and, yes, self-assured. You certainly have your views on things and will find it difficult to change your perspective even if others give you a good reason to do so.

You have a strong need to feel contented and in control of the situation you're in. In every aspect of your life it's important to you to stick with the tried and tested rather than impulsively stepping out of what you know and feel comfortable with. Moving in a new direction is not impossible, but you need very good reasons for doing so before taking a step forward. If others see the logic in some sort of change and you don't, this can become very frustrating for them.

Taurus encompasses practicality and a common-sense approach to life and relationships. Your star sign has the earth element and your personality reflects this perfectly. Such descriptions as prudent and tight-fisted don't worry you because you're primarily concerned about your future security and the wellbeing of your loved ones, especially if you're a parent.

When it comes to making big life changes you're extremely careful of how this might affect your family, especially if you're a person with children or others who are dependent upon you. You don't want your decisions to be impetuous and cause trouble for anyone, so you see caution and thoroughness as absolutely essential. Those who judge you harshly often overlook this fact and, if they realised just how attentive you are to the needs of others, they would realise that your decisions are usually based on a very sound footing.

You're one of the best workers an employer could have with them because you are meticulous about the way you do things. You're careful, never rush and, although you may not be the first to cross the finishing line with deadlines, your work is always first-rate. You hate cutting corners and doing more than one thing at a time. If you're forced to rush it really increases your stress levels because you know that doing a job well requires complete focus and attention, and this you have.

Because you need to be in control of things, those who work and live with you need to understand that you can't be pushed or shoved. When the bull digs in its heels, no one on Earth can move it. You probably relate to this quite well as I write it.

Change is sometimes a fearful thing for Taurus so this is one of your biggest challenges in life. Try to go with the flow more and don't be afraid to listen to others who may see an angle that you don't. Usually your inflexibility is based on the most trivial and unimportant thing, so try practising being open in your responses before venturing to make those big life changes that are a little scary.

Venus, which governs Taurus, reflects your taste for artistic things and a luxurious lifestyle. You enjoy all of the good things that money can buy, including fine food and drink, but don't let the excessive side of this planet overrun your life. Your health and wellbeing may suffer if you overdo it.

You're a sensitive and patient individual and will wait for success even if it takes longer than it does for others. To you, slow and steady wins the race. You understand the value of hard work. You only accept opportunities if you can see some practical value in them.

You have a simple yet graceful charm that others find alluring. You possess natural beauty that doesn't need embellishment. You also have strong intuition to trust your instincts because your judgement of others is often correct.

Three classes of Taurus

If you were born between the 21st and the 29th of April you're endowed with huge amounts of affection due to the influence of Venus. This means your love life and romance is extremely important to you. One of your main life lessons is that bigger and better does not always equate with happiness. Attracting someone of means shouldn't be the criteria for whether or not you want to spend the rest of your life with them.

If you were born between the 30th of April and the 10th of May, Mercury stimulates your mind and makes you severely critical of yourself and others. Try to balance your reasoning with your intuition and this will bring you considerably more contentment in life.

If you were born between the 11th and the 21st of May you're interested in finance, money and material acquisitions that give you power over others. Being practical and saving for your long-term objectives is a key feature of your personality, but don't forget to use your power wisely.

Taurus role model: Queen Elizabeth II

The Queen of England Elizabeth II epitomises the earthy no-nonsense approach of Taurus. The Queen never minces words and even seems a little dour at times *but* she has executed her duty with 100 per cent dedication. The Queen is also a stickler for detail and never cuts corners when dealing with even the most trivial tasks.

Taurus: The light side

Venus is a very social planet and therefore you're seen to be an engaging character who loves life and loves to be with people. You've got a great sense of humour and never look down on others. Even if you happen to climb the social ladder you never forget your roots. You treat everyone equally and this is one of your greatest assets.

You have wonderful artistic skills even if you're not an artist, per se. You're born with a natural flair for art, craft and a sense of colour, form and beauty. Anything fine-looking attracts you and likewise the beauty in you attracts others.

You exhibit a no-frills approach when it comes to helping others and your words are honest and cut straight to the heart of the problem. People look to you for assistance when they are in trouble. You're kind, sensible and your help is always positive.

You display a great work ethic, which is commendable. Your basic philosophy is that even the smallest task should be carried out with care and precision. You're a perfectionist in your own way. Share your talents with others, even though you're modest. Others can learn from you.

Taurus: The shadow side

It is important for you to delegate tasks and trust that others can do things as well as you. If you're able to do this you will be astounded at the amount of time you save.

You're too stubborn for your own good sometimes, and sooner or later you will realise that it pays to be more flexible, if only to keep the peace.

On the home front Taurus is the boss but sometimes is way too bossy, I might add. As long as everything is working to your plan you will be happy; but as soon as someone decides that they need to take control, it can throw a spanner in the works and upset you considerably.

Others are annoyed by the fact that your philosophy is often 'my way, or the highway'. You must let others grow and develop their own abilities so that you don't come across as being a control freak.

One of your greatest traits is determination, but if you take this to the extreme, it will only serve to push others away. You need to be honest with yourself to change these ingrained habits.

Taurus woman

Taurus women are upstanding, goal orientated and practical to the nth degree. They are extremely determined and never let anything get in the way of their ambitions. Once you have set your mind on something, nothing stops you from obtaining it. You're practical and have a commonsense approach to achieving your objectives.

Hard work is your second name and others' opinions don't necessarily worry you because you believe in yourself. You're dedicated towards getting results, even though it may be done at a slower and steadier pace than others. Patience is another one of your virtues.

You understand that sometimes, because the planet Venus rules you, the feminine qualities of this planet are fully evident in your character. Softness and grace are part of your Taurean temperament as well as your physical expression.

Because Venus also rules fashion, makeup and grooming, you're quite conscious of cleanliness and are instinctively tasteful and elegant in the way you dress—but not flashy. As long as an outfit is comfortable and pleasing to the eye you'll wear it.

You have an attractive way about you and know how to dress for the occasion even though most of the time you enjoy hanging about in jeans and possibly even bare feet. The earth is dear to your heart and you love to get as close to it as you can, sometimes even at the expense of looking like a million bucks.

Family life is very important. Taurean women make excellent home-makers and mothers. Having children is one of your primary ambitions in life. Once you have children, you will be protective, loving and focused in doing your duty to the best of your ability as a parent.

You have a nurturing attitude and this makes you a great cook, and an excellent hostess for friends and visitors. Your house is your pride and joy and creating a secure and stable home life really makes you feel fulfilled in life.

Whether you're a professional woman or a home-maker, having a plan and working to that schedule are imperative. You don't necessarily like doing things off-the-cuff because this throws you into the deep end and makes you feel as if you're losing control. You like to know the how, where, when and why of life to feel comfortable.

You're a focused individual but this focus usually functions best with one task at a time. You don't like being distracted and multi-tasking is not your forte. If you set your mind to something, you dislike people steering you off your course. People are surprised at the fact that you're not scared to get your hands dirty on a job in one instance, and then find you turning around the next minute looking absolutely fabulous.

Taurean women are opinionated and often stubborn in their views, and this is one area that you will need to work on to improve your relation-ships and the general flow of your life.

Taurus man

Men born under Taurus are usually quite rugged, outgoing types who love nature and earthy practical activities. Although Venus is a feminine planet, Taurean men are extremely masculine in everything they do.

Don't expect men of this star sign to be showy, fast or the centre of attention. They prefer a slow, plodding and efficient expression of their energy.

If you're born under Taurus you prefer material security to anything else and this is what makes you feel secure within.

You're a loyal individual and in your relationships you're a one-on-one type of person. Women do find you attractive but at times you're a little slow off the mark and need to 'suss things out' before giving your heart fully to another person.

You have a traditional flavour about you and could even be described as a little old-fashioned in your views, but you're caring and loving, even if you're not always as demonstrative as your partner would like. You value friends and family and do what you can to make them feel safe, secure and protected. You're able to shoulder huge responsibilities better than most others because, when you make a commitment to someone or some objective, you don't deviate.

You're a very high achiever in life but you like to take your time and savour each and every step of the journey. You like the good old-fashioned way of doing a job as best as you can so that you don't later have to cover up your mistakes.

You do have a creative element to your personality; however, this is not always obvious or superficial. Your innate creativity is found in the practical tasks that you do.

You have an amazing amount of commitment in achieving your goals and you only have to look at the huge number of successful people born under your star sign to see just how much success Taurus is capable of.

Children love fathers born under Taurus because they are always there as a support for them. Providing material and emotional support whenever it's needed is second nature to you and, even though you may be somewhat tough and inflexible in raising them, they will always know that you love them with all of your heart.

You need to be consultative in your relationships when making decisions. Try to express your feelings a little more, even if you don't agree with your partner. Sometimes Taurean men become a little closed emotionally and this is usually because they harbour some fears for their future security.

By talking about these issues you will be surprised at just how much better you will feel knowing that your partner wants to take part of that load off your shoulders.

Taurus child

The child of Taurus is a huge ball of love and affection and that's because Venus, the sweet planet, showers them with these wonderfully endearing qualities. They have a natural charm as well as a humorous streak, which makes them irresistibly lovable.

Your Taurus child is cuddly but doesn't necessarily show this the way other children do. They sit back, wait, and respond once you stimulate them.

They also are a little slow off the mark when it comes to taking action so you need to be there to give them that extra nudge of encouragement, coupled with some emotional nurturing. If you pay attention to their shifting moods, which are not always evident on the surface, you will see they actually have much more energy than they're prepared to show you.

Taurus is a touchy-feely sign and therefore your Taurean child does crave physical and emotional affection. You need to display your love to them, otherwise they may feel unloved and unworthy. Physical contact in particular is essential for them because Taurus is a tactile sign.

The Taurean child is an excellent sales person in that when they want something they will get it and they never give up until you cave in. A battle of wills is likely if you resist them, so you need to learn the art of negotiation with these young, often demanding characters.

Taurean children love the world and being outdoors, playing with animals and nature. This is essential for their all-round development.

Hopefully you have a garden or some natural arena in which you can share time together. This is an excellent tonic for their souls and will help them mature in a balanced way.

Although Taurean children have an active and artistic imagination they are also well suited to maths, science and geography. You will find music is also an excellent activity, which they take to naturally. Their hearts and minds will be well benefited, especially if they have a brooding disposition. Encourage these artistic activities and hobbies for them.

Your Taurus child will have a large group of friends as he or she grows older and will more than likely be the centre of attention. They need to learn the art of sharing because they are possessive of their toys and other valuables. Guide your children well and teach them the art of flexibility and forgiveness. By doing so, you will help them become the best they can be.

Romance, love and marriage

Don't bother falling in love with a Taurus if you're only after a temporary affair or a casual one-night stand. Taurus is anything but casual in love and once your heart meets theirs you will realise just how devoted and intense their affection and commitment can be.

You will need to give Taurus reassurances that your love includes nurturing, protecting and securing the future for them. If you were born under Taurus you will know exactly what I mean when I say that friendship, companionship and working together as a team is as important as the sexual aspects of your relationship.

A durable relationship in which your family is the pivotal focus is part and parcel of your ideal of love. Taurus is one of the most nurturing signs of the zodiac and therefore you'll easily fit into the role of homemaker and parent. This seems to come so naturally to you. Your partner needs to understand that family life is the key to your romantic happiness.

You're not a greedy person but you like the idea of falling in love with someone who is practical and able to provide you with the things in life that make for a comfortable lifestyle. You see their financial input—contributing to the bills, helping around the house, etcetera—as the yardstick by which you measure their commitment to you.

You're a patient individual and may have to wait a little longer than most to find the right person. The person of your dreams is no light affair for you. You have a reasonably high benchmark as to what constitutes a good soulmate.

You're honest as the day is long but you're also single-minded in making it clear about what you want. Loyalty, fidelity and traditional values appeal to you.

Your Taurean love is possessive in many ways and this can make it difficult for your relationships if your partner happens to be a more easygoing type of person who likes to socialise with others. You should be mature enough to offer your partner independence and freedom for their personal growth as well.

If you do happen to find your soulmate you regard this as an important responsibility and expect the same measure of seriousness in return. Try to cherish the love you have but at the same time don't slip into too much of a routine, which will create a sense of boredom.

Taurus does tend to stagnate in some cases and the thrill of romance could slip away from you. Work hard at paying attention to your lover by remaining youthful and communicative about how you feel.

Keeping a tight rein over your emotions is based upon your earlier mistrust of others when some of your relationships didn't work out. Let the past go and look to the future with a fresh approach so that you can demonstrate your love to your partner, thus ensuring an ever-fresh experience for you.

You're one of the most sensual signs of the zodiac, therefore your partner will be fortunate when it comes to sex and moments of intimacy. In fact, there are times where excessive pleasure and experimentation may be detrimental to your health. Try to moderate all of your activities and keep a balance, even in your pursuit of romantic pleasure.

Nature will be a key factor in reviving your feelings of love in a relationship. Spend time away from your regular residence and re-charge your romantic batteries with your spouse or partner. This will ensure that your love remains vital and forever fresh.

Health, wellbeing and diet

The earthy sign of Taurus is physically strong and resilient. You're able to live a long, strong and healthy life as long as you don't over indulge your taste for fine food, alcohol, and late nights partying. Moderation is a key component of your ongoing health and vitality.

You do have a tendency to gain weight, especially later in life, so get into the habit of counting those calories earlier rather than later. Many Taureans have a sweet tooth, which is one of the main culprits of this weight gain.

The sign of Taurus rules the throat, mouth, neck and face and therefore these parts of your body may from time to time cause you some discomfort. Tonsils, thyroid, the parathyroid and upper spinal vertebrae, jaw and mouth are constitutionally weak points. A thyroid problem could cause you to feel very lethargic and unenthusiastic. If in doubt, consult with your health practitioner.

Dental hygiene also falls under the rulership of Taurus and hints at the need to eat simple and easily digestible meals. Also, another good idea is to pay attention to poor food combinations, which can cause indigestion and other digestive problems.

Eat slowly, don't overeat, and you will be surprised at how most foods will be tolerated by your Taurean temperament as a result.

Work

Work and Taurus are a natural fit. Being an earthy sign, practical and financial activities seem to be the best possible way for you to relax yourself as well as earning a substantial nest egg for later in life.

Being naturally drawn to work, you're attentive and efficient in fulfilling your responsibilities and will be found to be honest and punctual in all your appointments and deadlines.

You like to take your time learning any new trade or career, but once you have taken in all the facts, you execute your work much more efficiently than most others.

Your employers will find you to be reliable and always trustworthy in your dealings. For this reason your employer will have no problem in handing over the responsibility of money to you. You're dependable and will never breach their trust.

Whether you work for yourself or for others you have a fine intuitive streak, which gives you a great sense of timing. This will serve you well and underpins much of your success.

As long as an idea can be executed with some material value as the end result, you will put 100 per cent of your energy and time into it, but anything that is unplanned or 'pie in the sky' will not at all appeal to you.

For you, Taurus, the best occupations are those that include the home, or house sciences, gardening and landscape design. Real estate is an excellent choice and Taurus also has an affinity with banking and insurance fields.

Due to your artistic leanings, interior design, architecture and fashion or retail could be a good fit. Makeup or hairstyling and other cosmetically related industries also find many Taureans gravitating towards these fields.

Key to karma, spirituality and emotional balance

The earth sign of Capricorn is ruled by Saturn and indicates your journey through your last life. These traits, although belonging to the sign of Capricorn, do have a marked influence on you. This star sign colours your karmic complexion. Your key words are 'I have' and so it is important not to let your desire for money and material ambition overshadow the more personal side of life.

Nature and the outdoors are excellent spiritual re-chargers for you. Try to get adequate walks and fresh air.

Try to relax more and not stress about how much you have or don't have. Meditations on Wednesdays will help this. Taking calming baths using sandalwood, cedarwood and rose oils will help connect you to your higher self. Jasmine oil is also an excellent tonic for your spirit.

Your lucky days

Your luckiest days are Wednesdays, Fridays and Saturdays.

Your lucky numbers

Remember that the forecasts given later in the book will help you optimise your chances of winning. Your lucky numbers are:

6, 15, 24, 33, 42, 51

5, 14, 23, 32, 41, 50

8, 17, 26, 35, 44, 53

Your destiny years

Your most important years are 6, 15, 24, 33, 42, 51, 60, 78 and 87.

Star Sign Compatibility

A *loving heart is the truest wisdom*.

—Charles Dickens

Romantic compatibility

How compatible are you with your current partner, lover or friend? Did you know that astrology can reveal a whole new level of understanding between people simply by looking at their star sign and that of their partner? In this chapter I'd like to share some special insights that will help you better appreciate your strengths and challenges using Sun sign compatibility.

The Sun reflects your drive, willpower and personality. The essential qualities of two star signs blend like two pure colours, producing an entirely new colour. Relationships, similarly, produce their own emotional colours when two people interact. The following is a general guide to your romantic prospects with others and how, by knowing the astrological 'colour' of each other, the art of love can help you create a masterpiece.

When reading the following I ask you to remember that no two star signs are ever *totally* incompatible. With effort and compromise, even the most 'difficult' astrological matches can work. Don't close your mind to the full range of life's possibilities! Learning about each other and ourselves is the most important facet of astrology.

Each star sign combination is followed by the elements of those star signs and the result of

Quick-reference guide: Horoscope compatibility between signs (percentage)

	Aries	Taurus	Gemini	Cancer	Leo	Virgo	Libra	Scorpio	Sagittarius	Capricorn	Aquarius	Pisces
Aries	60	65	65	65	90	45	70	80	90	50	55	65
Taurus	60	70	70	80	70	90	75	85	50	95	80	85
Gemini	70	70	75	60	80	75	90	60	75	50	90	50
Cancer	65	80	60	75	70	75	60	95	55	45	70	90
Leo	90	70	80	70	85	75	65	75	95	45	70	75
Virgo	45	90	75	75	75	70	80	85	70	95	50	70
Libra	70	75	90	60	65	80	80	85	80	85	95	50
Scorpio	80	85	60	95	75	85	85	90	80	65	60	95
Sagittarius	90	50	75	55	95	70	80	85	85	55	60	75
Capricorn	50	95	50	45	45	95	85	65	55	85	70	85
Aquarius	55	80	90	70	70	50	95	60	60	70	80	55
Pisces	65	85	50	90	75	70	50	95	75	85	55	80

their combining. For instance, Aries is a fire sign and Aquarius is an air sign and this combination produces a lot of 'hot air'. Air feeds fire and fire warms air. In fact, fire requires air. However, not all air and fire combinations work. I have included information about the different birth periods within each star sign and this will throw even more light on your prospects for a fulfilling love life with any star sign you choose.

Good luck in your search for love, and may the stars shine upon you in 2010!

Compatibility quick-reference guide

Each of the twelve star signs has a greater or lesser affinity with one another. The quick-reference guide will show you who's hot and who's not so hot as far as your relationships are concerned.

TAURUS + ARIES
Earth + Fire = Lava

It's quite likely that your involvement with an Aries will find you both locking horns. The ram, with their horns, and you, Taurus, with your horns, are likely to go at it head first, on many occasions.

Aries is much more direct, wilful and reactive, but they will soon learn that although you don't often speak your mind in the first instance, if they push you too hard, they are soon likely to see the explosive nature of your bullish temperament.

You find it difficult to reconcile Aries' stop—start temperament because you're very determined and stick to your guns, no matter what. The Arian spontaneity will spark an interest and excite you; but on a practical level, this could jeopardise your security consciousness. You will need to spend considerable time re-educating Aries in this area of life, especially where money is concerned.

For both of you, control is a very important issue but you have a less obvious way of expressing this than Aries. You're more level-headed and like to do things one step at a time. For you, this helps you set up a foundation in life and create something of lasting value. Aries has a very different approach and likes the confrontational path, which is a little like 'all, or nothing at all'.

If you find yourself drawn to Aries born between the 21st and the 30th of March, there could be problems financially. You don't want to end up carrying the burden of their financial mismanagement. You need someone who is more responsible with the dollars and cents.

I see exceptionally good relationships with Aries born between the 31st of March and the 10th of April, mainly because Leo also has an influence on them. This will affect the domestic satisfaction and thus promises to be a very good match. With these Aries being extremely charming, it is going to be hard for you not to be attracted to them.

Those Aries born between the 11th and the 20th of April will be a little too wild and ambitious for your temperament. You like someone a little more down to Earth than they are.

TAURUS + TAURUS
Earth + Earth = Solid Ground

You don't only lock horns with Aries: obviously another Taurus has the same horns as you do. Therefore you could also find yourself being 'entangled' emotionally with another Taurean and challenged by their stubbornness, which is just as entrenched as yours.

Although both of you are very honest and direct in your dealings with each other, neither of you tends to be flexible enough in your opinions to give in. However, the one saving grace is that you both have a very similar view on life and the way your day-to-day life should be lived.

The Taurus–Taurus combination can definitely work because you're both very loving and sensual beings and like to nurture each other. This affection will be mutually appreciated and gives you both a sense that you understand each other's needs deeply. As long as you can learn the value of being flexible and adapting to each other's more subtle needs, the lesson you learn will help both of you make this relationship even better.

Because neither of you likes to change too easily, it will be difficult for this relationship to grow spiritually. One of you will need to be the initiator so that your time together will help you both develop as people. Because of this there is a strong level of complacency, which in the extreme, might I even say, can be laziness in a double-Taurus match.

You both need security, lots of money and a safe haven, and this you can and will provide to each other. Don't let your individual work regimes intrude on your personal lives. This could be another reason for the relationship bogging down and not reaching its full potential. Usually, though, a Taurus and Taurus combination brings with it the promise of a happy home life, strong domestic bonds and long-term financial and emotional security.

If you're looking for the perfect Taurean as your partner, look no further than those born between the 21st and the 29th of April. You will certainly feel a deep association with them and this partnership will go far.

With Taurus individuals born between the 30th of April and the 10th of May I can see loads of romance and fun-filled times. Your sexual intimacy will be one of the notable highs of a relationship with them.

With Taureans born between the 11th and the 21st of May, I see a really great working relationship that will satisfy your financial needs, but whether this is enough to give you the lifelong emotional fulfilment you need is the question.

TAURUS + GEMINI
Earth + Air = Dust

Your ruling planets are friendly—that is Venus, which rules you, and Mercury, which rules Gemini. This is always a great start in either a friendship or a more romantic association and, even though your personal styles are very different, you can enjoy each other's company and probably make this relationship work quite well.

You, Taurus, are much slower than your Gemini counterpart and therefore either you need to step up the pace or they need to slow things down a little so that you can both meet each other halfway.

In terms of communication, Gemini is fast paced, with lightning-speed mental and physical reactions. They like to draw their conclusions very quickly and this threatens you in some ways because you would far prefer to take your time weighing up the pros and cons of any situation before coming to a firm decision.

Once you do make up your mind it is rare for you to change it. This could bother Gemini, who is very flexible and seeks change from day to day. This might present you with lifestyle issues because it's important for you to find security in the tried and tested. Gemini will find this rather boring and so the challenge for you will be to create a nurturing environment that doesn't unsettle you but at the same time gives Gemini enough variety to keep them interested.

Although many astrologers point out the 'schizo-phrenic' and scattered personality types of Gemini, the truth is they are quite versatile individuals with an immense amount of intelligence and imagina-tion. You too will find that they are deeper than they appear on the surface, if you can give them a little bit more of an opportunity to display it.

Taurus and Gemini are sexually compatible in an unusual sort of way but Gemini will more than likely have to be the initiator. With their curious and inventive minds they will stimulate your desire to explore the sensual side of your Taurean nature and will be able to take you to a new level of pleasure and sensual enjoyment.

Geminis born between the 22nd of May and the 1st of June will get on well with you and offer you a different sort of lifestyle to that which you're accustomed. As with any typical Gemini, you can expect long and entertaining chats with them, which attracts you to them.

Geminis born between the 2nd and the 12th of June are really well suited to you because your own ruling planet Venus holds sway over them. As well as being extremely intelligent and conversational, they also possess great aesthetic and cultural taste, too.

There are a class of Geminis born between the 13th and the 21st of June and if you choose to team up with them, you should expect life to be quite exciting, if not hectic. If you're a typical Taurean and like to maintain a fixed routine, these Geminis will most probably challenge you as they are very spontaneous in the way they live life.

TAURUS + CANCER
Earth + Water = Mud

Taurus and Cancer are very well suited to each other and this will be evident the moment you discover just how sensitive and caring they are. It is as if Cancer truly understands what the word 'nurturing' means, and this is one very important aspect of their personalities that they bring to a relationship with Taurus.

In connecting with this caring and loving side of Cancer, you will see a part of your own emotional nature reflected in the mirror of their personality. You might not need to look too much further than Cancer to feel truly satisfied in a relationship.

Although the affectionate Cancer instinctively realises what you need, you will have to be prepared for their very moody and changeable character. Your steadfast influence will be beneficial in helping them bring their minds to a more stable position. They look up to you for your power of endurance and also your loyalty.

There is a great social connection between Taurus and Cancer as well. Taurus happens to be the eleventh zodiac sign to Cancer, which relates to social life and true friendship. The two of you make a great team both on the home front and on the social scene as well.

This is a great combination for family life and will bring you both a great deal of satisfaction in the long-term. You're extremely supportive of each other and your family life should in most cases work like a well-oiled machine.

Being an emotional water sign, Cancer brings to the table a vast amount of spiritual and calming wisdom along with a touch of psychic insight. This will intrigue you and Cancer at some point in your relationship will definitely help you progress in your own spiritual endeavours.

Excitement and sexual attraction draw you together. The feminine planets of Venus and the Moon govern both of you respectively and so your physical needs will be sparked by your emotional connection to each other.

Cancer is idealistic, compassionate and loves to help others, at their own expense sometimes. Don't count the pennies when you see Cancer giving help to someone, even a stranger, because this gives them great satisfaction. If the more materialistic side of your nature comes to the fore they will feel as if you're denying them one of life's great pleasures, which is to give.

Generally Taurus and Cancer are quite compatible, but a relationship with Cancerians born between the 22nd of June and the 3rd of July is even better. I see a sensitive and loving match between the two of you. One of you will have to play the hero if the relationship starts to 'wash out' with sentimentality, though.

You're very attracted to Cancerians who are born between the 4th and the 13th of July. These people are co-ruled by Mars, which is your marital planet. Obviously a relationship with someone born during this cycle should grow into something special and would be a good marriage combination.

If you have your eye on a Cancer born between the 14th and the 23rd of July, friendship is more ideally suited to you both rather than any deep, sexual relationship. Although you'll have a strong attraction for each other there will be something lacking and for you that sexual aspect is essential if you're to feel comfortable.

TAURUS + LEO
Earth + Fire = Lava

A Taurus–Leo love relationship can be very special, indeed. With you being ruled by Venus and the Sun ruling the showy Leo, this mix of earth and fire elements is hot property as far as romances are concerned. You will feel an instant attraction for each other and those around you will also notice this when in your company, too.

Your Leo friend is dramatic, exciting and likes to take to the floor and be the centre of attention. You're certainly attractive in your own way but this type of attention seeking is not your forte. You will let Leo bathe in the limelight but at the same time you will love their vitality, warmth and social inter-action. The Leo personality really does turn you on.

Being with them will cause you to see that life is indeed a stage and that we are all playing our parts. Leo of course will probably take the leading role.

Leo will have to understand that being in a relationship with you requires commitment and compromise. The commitment aspect may not be the problem here, however, because Leo is one of the most loyal signs of the zodiac. It is the compromise part that could bog you down because they are very self-centred and probably as opinionated as you.

Leo is protective of family and loved ones and is committed to providing comfort and financial security, which is another part of their character that you really like. You will have no problem creating a safe haven for your family but, as I said, you will need to both be flexible enough to allow each other to think the way you do and to respect each other for that.

You have a very powerful sexual connection with Leo but I suggest you don't rush things in the first stages and get to know each other on a mental level as well. Your pleasurable pursuits together will mature over time and, the other positive aspect of your relationship is that once the initial excitement of your sexual lovemaking tones down, you will still find considerable amount of satisfaction in other areas of life.

Leos born between the 24th of July and the 3rd of August have much in common with you and make great partners. You both like the idea of family and a soft place to land in the family sense. These Leo-born individuals will protect and nurture you and you will feel comfortable in your support for them in everything they do.

Take some precautions with those born between the 4th and the 13th of August. We all know how money and security conscious Taurus is and there's nothing worse for you than unnecessary risks. These people will be spendthrifts who make you feel quite uncomfortable on a material level. But they do come up with some amazing concepts for business and, if you're prepared for the odd gamble, their wacky schemes might just pay off, to your and their satisfaction.

With Leos born between the 14th and the 23rd of August, I see much passion added to an already general compatibility between you. Mars dominates them and this will at times create some turbulent episodes. Relationships for you need to be a two-way street and you will find these individuals taking more than they give.

TAURUS + VIRGO
Earth + Earth = Solid Ground

Taurus and Virgo is a winning combination astrologically and I might even say nearly perfect. Both signs fall under the same elemental category of earth, which means you're perfectly suited on many levels and will feel attracted to each other from day one.

Virgo is practical and down to earth like you are. You rely a little more on gut instinct in this respect but will admire the incredibly detailed mindset of your Virgo partner. To an extent, you will find it difficult to meet their high standards and they can be rather critical at times, not just of you, but of themselves as well. They have a habit of never being satisfied with what you do and, because they are rather quick and efficient in achieving their goals, you might find yourself lagging behind them, feeling somewhat judged.

Virgo will never hold back in telling you what they feel. On the one hand you will feel great about their honesty but the downside is that they may be a little too honest for your liking. You will hear about every detail of where you can improve what you have done wrong and how it should have been done like this or that, so you will need to muster up plenty of your Taurean patience when discussing these issues because the Virgo mentality can be challenging at times.

You will soon learn that Virgo is also one of the most delicate and sensitive signs of the zodiac. They can 'dish it out', but they cannot always take it back as easily. They will react strongly if you choose to point out some of their faults, so be very careful when and if you also criticise them, because their thin skin will leave them battered and bruised. In a way you will find this quite amusing.

Both of you have eclectic tastes and love all sorts of art, fashion, music and other crafts and practical activities. There is plenty of mutual enjoyment together. Make sure you teach Virgo the art of relaxation so that their busy minds and frazzled nerves don't cause them to overwork and suffer health problems.

Virgo is more romantic than people first believe and once you stimulate them you will see they can bring some very interesting and imaginative insights into your sexual relationship. Your affinity on this level will also fuel the fire of your love for each other and overcome any shortcomings you feel between you.

Virgos born between the 24th of August and the 2nd of September are very playful, sensual and sexual in nature. You are very comfortable with them and therefore you feel as if your relationship will be straightforward and honest without too many barriers between you.

Virgos born between the 3rd and the 12th of September have a serious side to their nature. They are very highly strung and volatile individuals and therefore you need to be a happy-go-lucky sort of Taurean if this relationship has a chance of survival.

All Virgos are attractive to you and they will feel the same. Those born between the 13th and the 22nd of September, however, better reflect your life ideals and your personal desires. There's a strong karmic and spiritual connection with these people and you will feel you have known them before, possibly in another life.

TAURUS + LIBRA
Earth + Air = Dust

Venus is the governor of both Taurus and Libra so you have much in common and will effortlessly find yourselves attracted to each other. Libra being an air sign has some fine intellectual qualities but your earth element might find them a little ungrounded. Libra will push hard for balance, but to gain their idea of balance, they may constantly push you in a direction you don't feel comfortable going.

It is not that you're not social, because you certainly enjoy each other's company and that of others, but Libra is the consummate social butterfly and that could drive them to place more importance on friends than on the relationship itself.

You need someone who can demonstrate to you their loyalty and give you the sense that you're number one on their list of priorities, not just another person in a long line of contacts and engagements that Libra has on its social agenda.

Libra understands that you have a need for security, but are you aware of just how much they need to communicate? Libra has a primary need to be in a relationship with someone who can share their feelings and not withhold love and attention. And, speaking of attention, Libra will demand it even when you're not in the mood, so you're going to have to 'step up to the plate' to satisfy what you consider to be excessive emotional demands from time to time.

However, Taurus and Libra work well together and if you're prepared to listen to their ideas they can help with your professional ambitions. Give them a chance to direct you. You're the financial anchor, and Libra is the creative fuel in this relationship.

You're both revitalised in each other's company but you will need to get out of any lethargic patterns. If you're a couch potato, make sure your choice of video is exciting and mentally stimulating.

As long as you can both adjust to each other's lifestyles by finding a happy medium, you will be able to accommodate each other's needs, which is what your relationship depends on. Even though your sexual connection will probably work well, it may not be enough to propel this relationship forward over the long term.

Those Librans born between the 24th of September and the 3rd of October are doubly ruled by Venus and their life goals will be very much in tune with yours. Your relationship with them looks set to be a beauty because you're so connected to each other.

Librans born between the 4th and the 13th of October are also associated with Uranus and Aquarius and therefore they have very fast-moving minds, which are sometimes a little off-beat as well. You could feel unstable or even insecure with them and will need time to think this one through a little more.

Librans born between the 14th and the 23rd of October are extremely attracted to you. They have sensuality oozing from every pore of their skin. You'll be attracted to this and it could become a very powerful relationship. Over and above your physical attraction to each other, communication will be strong and your social skills will definitely need to be sharpened to keep up with them.

TAURUS + SCORPIO
Earth + Water = Mud

Taurus and Scorpio are opposite signs of the zodiac and it is a well-known astrological fact that opposite signs do attract. You, Taurus, with Venus ruling you, and Scorpio with Mars and Pluto driving them to passion and intensity, will find yourselves karmically drawn to each other. You cannot deny the palpable sensations you feel in each other's company. Not all opposite signs of the zodiac are as compatible but the Taurus–Scorpio mix is one that stands at the top of the list of relationships that have the power of endurance.

Scorpios communicate in silence but if you look closely enough you will see that their eyes speak much more about what is going on within their hearts and their minds. Initially their steely exterior might make you a little confused about how they feel about you. Soon enough, however, you will realise that they have an intense passion for you and may even become obsessive about their love for you. This Venus and Mars combination is the classic love match and the connection between you is undeniable.

Because you're both fixed star signs, you're stubborn, and this is a trait both of you need to overcome if you would like the more positive aspects of this relationship to shine. Enjoying this relationship will not always be easy because Taurus and Scorpio are often engaged in a battle of wills for control over many issues in their lives. Understanding is always the key and in this combination humility will play an even more important role.

The deep sexual and emotional power of Scorpio and their ability to make you the focus of this power will elevate you to the level of a god or goddess, but sooner or later you will realise that Scorpio demands as much as it gives in love. You may be up to the task intermittently but the Scorpio demand is relentless and, irrespective of how compatible your star signs are, this can eventually wear you down if you're not a resilient and tough type of Taurean.

Scorpios are by far the most sexual star sign and you're not too badly endowed with this quality, either. Therefore this is definitely a powerful and long-lasting combination that has at its heart a deep bond of love and sexual attractiveness linking both of you together.

You can also handle financial and practical concerns well together and, once you find out and agree who will play which role in the relationship, the two of you can be a formidable financial pair. The Taurus and Scorpio couple builds a good base of material stability from which to springboard into a harmonious and equally stable family life.

Many Scorpios get on extremely well with you, but those born between the 24th of October and the 2nd of November are even better suited, as far as I'm concerned. You're compatible emotionally, mentally, sexually and, most importantly, spiritually. You can safely make long-term plans and commit yourself to them.

Scorpios born between the 3rd and the 12th of November are better suited to you as friends rather than lovers. You do, however, have good spiritual and karmic bonds with them and I anticipate some unusual and memorable experiences for the two of you. These Scorpios spin beautiful romantic dreams, which may enamour you but could be a little too impractical for your Taurean commonsense.

If you're considering a Scorpio born between the 13th and the 22nd of November you mustn't expect anything other than moderately compatible results. They are extremely sensitive individuals whose moods shift like the tides. If you prefer emotionally stable partners, they may not be the ones to satisfy you.

TAURUS + SAGITTARIUS
Earth + Fire = Lava

Taurus and Sagittarius don't always agree and this is to be expected because you're both very different people whose life philosophies are at a variance. You live in a world where touching, feeling and seeing is believing. Sagittarius aspires to the same things but extends this view of life to include the spiritual and philosophical as well.

You have a grounded sort of character whereas Sagittarius is often found to be very footloose and fancy-free. This could be a concern for you, even if you're attracted to them, which you probably will be because they are very endearing and attractive people. In fact, some of them can be quite charismatic and will sweep you of your feet before you can realise the fact that the rock-solid security you look for may not be found in the Sagittarian individual.

As I have mentioned on many occasions, Taurus loves honesty, but will you be prepared for the brutal honesty of Sagittarius? Direct, even bluntly straight to the point, the way they express themselves can rub you the wrong way.

Anything that is crude or abrasive to you is not something you want as part of your life. How do you reconcile this rather different or extreme aspect of behaviour in Sagittarius? On the one hand they are charming and magnetic, yet on the other, they are blunt and egotistical.

Sagittarius is more adaptable than Taurus. They are what is known as a mutable sign, while you are a fixed sign. In short, you find it hard to adjust to the freedom-loving Sagittarian. If you can open your mind and heart just a little, you will discover a whole new dimension to life and this relationship can therefore be much more enjoyable and helpful to you than you realise.

Take care with Sagittarians born between the 23rd of November and the 1st of December as your luck will be adversely affected by them. Money is a problem for them when they don't respect it. If you do find yourself in a relationship with them, you need to be clear about where you stand on money matters. Don't let money come between you.

If you're looking for a soulmate within the Sagittarian ranks, you needn't look any further than those born between the 2nd and the 11th of December. Also being influenced by Aries and Mars, you're likely to share some wild and exciting times with them. Mars does, however, make them antagonistic and impulsive. This can be overwhelming because it impacts upon their ability to save money and this is something that will unnerve you.

Those born between the 12th and the 22nd of December bring with them lots of fun, humour and camaraderie. You'll have a great time with them and will be seen as an attractive couple. Going out at night and mixing with mutual friends will underpin your relationship. These Sagittarians will look after you and are not afraid to show their appreciation.

TAURUS + CAPRICORN
Earth + Earth = Solid Ground

Capricorn is as attracted to Taurus as you are to them. When you meet them you will be impressed by their down-to-earth and practical nature. Sound familiar? Of course! This reflects your own Taurean practicality and no-nonsense approach to life. You will each be naturally drawn to the other's common-sensical way of seeing and expressing things.

Capricorn is the most traditional of the star signs and is probably even a little more conservative than Taurus. This does not bother you because your basic drive is material security and Capricorn will more than satisfy these essential needs of yours. You find this very appealing, even if they are not the most exciting person to be with.

The fact that Capricorn can support the life-style you want makes you feel comfortable being around them. And although, as I just mentioned, their exuberance, enthusiasm and passion may not be traits that are initially evident, given time you will see that these characteristics are in fact part of Capricorn's nature but may be buried way deep inside them. This is where your ingenuity in drawing them out of themselves will be a challenge for you, Taurus.

Capricorn is a movable or changeable sign and so they do like to try new things occasionally, but they will need your push for them to do it. That may be asking a bit too much because you like your comforts and don't like change all that much unless it is absolutely necessary. The problem here is that you may both develop apathy for change if your Capricorn partner is a particularly conventional individual.

Capricorns born between the 23rd of December and the 1st of January are compatible with you. If you're interested in finance and material security they'll offer it to you. They are extremely hard workers and will provide for you and the family; not just the essentials of life but the luxuries as well. Your professional and financial goals are in keeping with each other.

Capricorns born between the 2nd and the 10th of January are really compatible with you. This is because they are co-ruled by your ruling planet Venus. These individuals are not as insular as the typical Capricorn and will also be surprisingly sensual. Venus makes them more demonstrative, which is ideal for what you're looking for. The two of you have a strong unspoken bond and this is a relationship that can endure.

A fine relationship can be expected with those born between the 11th and the 20th of January. This too can be a perfect love match because they are quite romantic individuals. They know how to win your heart and this is due to Mercury's influence. There is a touch of Virgo in them, which adds perfection to their style but don't forget, as with true Virgos, a touch of criticism as well.

TAURUS + AQUARIUS
Earth + Air = Dust

Aquarius is an extraordinary challenge for you, Taurus. While you are very practical and maybe traditional or even old-fashioned in some aspects of your life, Aquarius will attempt to blast this apart as soon as you lay eyes on them. Your contrasting views on life and the way you want to live it will be very obvious once you start dating them. Aquarius will constantly challenge you, demanding that you change and revolutionise your way of looking at things.

Taurus is not averse to change or improving the status quo; it is just that Aquarius may want you to do it just a little too quickly for your liking. You will have to inform them that change is something that needs to occur gradually in your life. If they don't get this concept then there is not much point in pursuing a relationship with them.

Aquarius is social, political, and community orientated, whereas you're more focused on the tangible and immediate aspects of your life. You have no problem in supporting causes, helping the downtrodden and sharing what you have with others, but not at the expense of your loved ones. You might find the Aquarian ideal a little weird when it comes to the way they share their love and maybe even their affection with all and sundry.

Both of you are fixed zodiac signs so your opinions are exactly that—a little stubborn and therefore self-centred to some extent. Being creatures of habit you will both stick to your guns and this could get worse as you get older.

Aquarius is unconventional in all matters of love, both sexually and in courtship. They may like to play the field and explore areas that you consider taboo. Yet again you will need to have an incredibly open mind to deal with their demands if you're to make this relationship work.

Be careful of Aquarians born between the 21st and the 31st of January. This is an unstable combination and you won't feel at all comfortable with their abrupt and avant-garde routine. There's an astrological joke alluding to the fact that Aquarians are sometimes at the heart of revolutions and political overthrows. Even if they aren't necessarily political, they will voice their opinions strongly, I can assure you.

You do, however, have quite a good connection with those Aquarians born between the 1st and the 9th of February. Mercury is a lucky planet for you and has a certain co-rulership over them. They have quick minds, a good sense of fun and you're therefore well suited.

Aquarians born between the 10th and the 19th of February have the touch of Venus and Libra and therefore reflect some of your Taurean qualities. This is a reasonably good match astrologically, but you will find it hard to deal with their changeable minds. Notwithstanding this, the future with them will be quite rosy.

TAURUS + PISCES
Earth + Water = Mud

Taurus and Pisces can be the best of buddies and your social 'friendship' and general camaraderie will be the dominating influence and connection between you.

Both of you value companionship, not just sex. Of course, you will be attracted to Pisces but you both appreciate that feeling comfortable with each other and being able to just hang out as friends is more important, especially in the later stages of a relationship.

You're drawn to the sensitive and spiritual side of Pisces. They don't seem to challenge your materialistic streak but there is a part of you that feels uncomfortable with such an idealistic approach to life. Pisces will in due course gently prod you to look beyond the practical affairs of life and consider the higher powers in nature and beyond. Their spiritual and humanitarian sensitivity will slowly wear down your earthly practicality, just like water on hardened soil. The elements of earth and water govern your life together.

Because you have such a natural grasp of practical things, this will be more than useful in helping Pisces come down to Earth and achieve something of value in their lives. Each of you helps balance the other's viewpoints and therefore, this relationship, if it is based on open and mutual love, can be a truly remarkable match. There is great scope for growth—emotionally, mentally and spiritually—for both of you.

I see a great meeting of the hearts and minds of those born between the 20th and the 28th or 29th of February. However, these individuals are truly visionary and see the world from another level, so you might find these people far too impracticable to sustain a long-term relationship with.

Pisces born between the 1st and the 11th of March are not really that compatible with you but they are responsive and emotional so it might be worth giving them a try. Teach them strength and decisiveness and don't dismiss them because they haven't developed these qualities to the same level as you. Practicality is a learned technique. Be their teacher.

Mars and Pluto dominate Pisceans born between the 12th and the 20th of March and this makes them powerful and intense individuals. They are seductive and exciting to be with as well as extraordinarily sexual, as you'll soon learn. These are the 'strong and silent' types and will be more demanding than you're prepared to accept. Unless you make some serious compromises you will not want to pursue a relationship with this type of Piscean.

2010:
The Year Ahead

*I recommend you take care of the minutes and the
hours will take care of themselves.*

—Earl of Chesterfield

Romance and friendship

There are times in your life when you're forced to
make significant choices and 2010 will certainly
be one of those times. The coming twelve months
present you with a choice between whether you're
finally prepared to assume responsibility for your
happiness in love, or be a victim of your circumstances.

With the presence of Mars in your zone of
domestic and family happiness, the early part of the
year and in particular January will be a confusing
time if you let it. You could make the serious mistake
of completely overlooking the fact that happiness is
to be found within yourself, not anywhere else.

Many of your personal ideals and beliefs over
romance, marriage and friendship will be completely
overhauled this year, especially as the solar eclipse
on the 15th of January takes place.

The other important omen after the 18th of
January is the entry of Jupiter, the benefactor, into
your zone of friendships and personal fulfilment.
With a deeper spiritual and emotional anchoring
underpinning your romantic and social life this year,
the presence of Jupiter will bring you happiness
without compromising your inner understanding
and wisdom.

Good feelings abound in February, even though Mars continues to backtrack to your important zone of relatives and closest family relationships. Issues surrounding your mother, father or nearest and dearest siblings will continue to present you with challenges, but by handling these with a 'can do' attitude, you will make significant inroads into releasing tension and fostering better feelings for the future.

After the 13th you need to be on guard that people aren't pushing your hot buttons and this is due to the presence of a Mercury and Mars combination. This is a time when you'll have to bring forth your strong and non-reactive Taurean side rather than the bull in your nature.

Towards the end of February you'll need to be careful not to allow rash behaviour to mar your relationships, or your health for that matter. You're likely to be irascible, temperamental and angry, and you'll certainly have some challenges.

This period of the year will continue to throw up challenges related to the way you have viewed relationships in the past and how you must now adjust to make the most of what life presents. If you dig in your heels and simply opt to stay with the known, the tried and to some extent the boring and unfulfilling, you'll miss some of the spectacular opportunities that Cupid is throwing your way.

Unfinished business in your life needs to be tackled and dealt with between April and July. Throughout this period Mars will finally make its forward movement through your domestic sphere and eventually make contact with Saturn in its reverse movement in your zone of children, creativity and love affairs. This could be a tense period in your life where unresolved feelings need to be expressed or at least directed in a way that is useful, not damaging. Did you know that depression and anxiety are often forms of unexpressed anger?

You mustn't let these aspects of your Taurean nature dominate your mind and heart. I have met many born under the sign of Taurus who suppress their feelings and then, when these planets come together, they find themselves at a loss of how to deal with the overwhelming power that is unleashed. So, having said this, I strongly advise that from April you open the lines of communication, talk to those you love or with whom you are havingproblems, and don't be afraid to seek counsel through your close network of friends or relatives who may be able to offer valuable advice during these trying months.

However, after reading this, against a backdrop of what appears to you to be a difficult time, I should give you some good news as well. Venus passing through your Sun sign in April makes you attractive and certainly desirable company for anyone whom you may have your eye upon.

There is some type of reconnection indicated in your horoscope during May and June. This is a time when you can seek out old friends or long-lost acquaintances; or strangely, karma itself may cause you to stumble upon some old and long-cherished friend. The past seems strong and feelings of nostalgia and sentimentality may overtake you throughout this period.

With your ruling planet Venus (and of course the planet of love) passing through your zone of travel in June, this is an opportune time to avail yourself of any invitation to get away and enjoy life in a completely different setting. You will have the chance to recharge your batteries and there is a real opportunity to meet new people from different cultures with diverse views and life goals. This could be a very inspiring time, indeed.

In August, Mercury and Venus transits your fifth zone of love affairs and this might even lead me to say that for some of you the choice between two lovers is a distinct possibility, even for those of you in a long-term, committed relationship. You can thank the complicated relationships of the planets Uranus, Jupiter, Venus, Saturn and Mars for this.

Venus and Mars associate with each other in September and October and it's likely that any attraction you have for someone in your workplace, or through some extra domestic or extracurricular activity, might flare up into a full-blown love affair. As long as your choices are made in good taste and you're prepared to wear the responsibility of the consequences of such hot and instinctive behaviour, I only have one thing to say to you: enjoy!

With the transit of the Sun conjoining Mercury and Venus in your marriage zone in late October and November, this is an ideal time to contemplate long-term relationships and to make that firm commitment if you're at marriageable age. This is a significant time of the year when many forces bear upon your biological and social needs and desires. Some of you may choose to settle down for a long-term relationship or possibly even become engaged to commit to the 'M' word; that is, marriage.

With the Moon also bringing out your nurturing instincts and defining itself in your fifth zone of children, anything associated with younger people—childbirth, motherhood, etcetera—will be spotlighted in this second last month of the year. The intense aspects from Pluto and your Sun sign to the Moon also show that your thinking and emotions will be very deep at this time. You won't be at all interested in any sort of superficiality, or nonsense associated with casual affairs or one-night stands. It really does appear that many Taureans are getting serious about their relationships during this very pivotal life cycle.

Towards the latter part of November, given these very striking planetary combinations, it should be noted that you mustn't make decisions on a knee jerk reaction or first impression. The danger when Mercury and Jupiter move into a difficult aspect after the 25th is that you may believe the embellished statements of someone else or you could exaggerate your own feelings and perceptions.

There is no rush, especially if you're planning to spend your whole life with someone, and I strongly recommend that you go a little slower, savour the moment, and learn as much as you can about the person that you may have fallen in love with (or feel that you have fallen in love with, anyhow).

December continues to showcase your talents in love and social life as Venus remains in your marriage zone. You may, however, feel somewhat bogged down by extra responsibilities at home or at work and not be fully able to appreciate your personal life for the first week or so of December. It appears your mind will be far away and therefore these responsibilities may also suggest you're concerned with self-improvement, which often requires some time out. You mustn't feel guilty about that, even if your friends are demanding more time than you have. Trust your instincts, make the time you need to get away, and spend some downtime decompressing and delving a little more deeply into your own needs and desires to see what you really want in life.

The lunar eclipse on the 21st of December is extremely important for Taurus because it takes place in your zone of finance and material values. Being an earthy and material sign, this should also encompass many of the values associated with your family, friendships, love and highest emotional ideals. If you have placed too much emphasis on what someone has, how much they earn and what they are able to provide you with in the world without adequately looking at the deeper spiritual side of this person, you may now find yourself seeing things in a completely different light. I hope so, because it is these deeper vibrations and energies that are going to reshape you in 2010 and make you a much more fulfilled person in love.

Work and money

As is your in-built nature, Taurus, you'll continue to work solidly to create more security and increased cash flow in 2010. The fact that you want to find out more about how to secure your future is shown by the presence of your ruling planet in the ninth zone of higher learning in January. This is significant by being conjoined with the Sun, Pluto and Mercury and shows that your mind is hungry for knowledge and any information that can help you better yourself in the material world throughout 2010.

In February you will immediately put to use what little new knowledge you have learned and can gain some immediate benefits in your working life. Your professional activities and your self-esteem are highly favoured due to Venus, the Sun and Neptune being located in the upper part or most important segment of your horoscope.

Mars sits in your zone of family and property until the middle of June and this strongly suggests that, while you may experience great opportunities in your professional life, it appears a delicate balance between your home life and your working life will create tension for you throughout the first half of the year and some confusion will result.

I said earlier that this is a year of challenges in which you must assume responsibility within yourself and not rely on external forces to shape your decisions and destiny. In your career, this perspective will also be a recurring theme throughout the coming twelve months. Try to use your intuition, develop trust in your own gut feelings, and the issues of which life path to take will be clearer to you.

You can meet important people throughout March and April when Venus, the Sun and Jupiter combine in your zone of friendships. Take full advantage of introductions and those windows of opportunity that come through social engagements, whether at work or away from your professional activities.

You may have to rely on charm rather than your wit or professional expertise in April. But don't feel guilty about that; when you're not feeling so flashy intellectually, at least you can fall back on your grace and other social skills to get you into the job or the situation required.

May, June and July are important months for earning more money, but also for learning how not to spend too much cash, particularly in July when your primary focus will be on property matters and getting the best deal for yourself in real estate.

Even if you have attained a good position, excellent money and considerable respect from your peers or employers, your karma is such that the period of August demands you dedicate some of your time to serving others. Sit down when I say this: you may have to give without any expectation of financial or material return. What, you say? The gains you achieve through this will be subtle and spiritual. Try to see beyond the remunerative value of what you do in your work at this time.

It seems as if you may have to put in some additional hours in your professional life and this may continue to the end of September or early October, during which period the Sun will also be moving through your sixth zone of work and service.

With the Sun conjoining with Saturn on the 1st of October in this same area, you're warned to guard against poor health stemming from excessive work practices, restless sleep and inadequate diet. Pay more attention to your vitamin intake and, of course, don't cut corners when it comes to your regular exercise. Mercury provides you some prime opportunities for communication with those who can improve your daily schedule after the 3rd.

Partnerships—whether they are associated with an independent business you carry on or simply in your work capacity as an employee—are favoured after the 20th of October when Mercury comes to your zone of public relations and partnerships. With Mars also creating an incredibly great aspect to your zone of profits and friendships on the 21st, this is the time to 'strike while the iron is hot'.

People who act as catalysts may come into the picture after the 23rd to help you secure some deal or to close off some contractual arrangement that has stalled, so don't worry if you feel as if things are sliding off the rails for a while. All will come good in time.

You mustn't delegate tasks to others that require your personal attention in November. This could be a serious mistake and may come back to haunt you down the track. If you sense something needs to be investigated more seriously, please do so because this will reveal to you further opportunities you had overlooked.

Don't be too serious about your work and money in December. Put your foot on the brake and allow yourself some downtime with some positive self-feedback. Give yourself a pat on the back and enjoy the results of your hard work without demanding too much more of yourself at the close of the year.

Karma, luck and meditation

The presence of your ruling planet and the Sun in the ninth zone of past karma is absolutely favourable for you and sets the tone for 2010 as being a lucky year, indeed.

The principal theme throughout the coming twelve months is that you have learned from your past mistakes and are now prepared to put them behind you and get on with life, accepting challenges without feeling you're a victim.

For many Taureans this is a time of incredible change. The Moon, your past karma point, Pluto, Venus, the Sun, Mercury and your future karma point are all together with Saturn in the movable signs. This means it's 'all systems go' for a transformative period.

In February your luck is assured in your working circumstances when the Sun and Venus conjoin in your zone of profession, ego and self-esteem. Some of you may be fortunate enough to receive a promotion or some great new position and this could even be unexpected but it is certainly well earned.

Your lucky months are February, March, August, October, November and December. During these months your ruling planet is in strong and friendly zones of the zodiac, offering you immense opportunities to further your luck and generate good karma for yourself.

Of course, for most people love is the primary source of happiness next to money, and passionate times are forecast for the period of October when your ruling planet Venus, and Mars come together in your significant zone of marriage.

Expect romance this year, particularly in the last three months of 2010. May the stars shine on you throughout the year.

2010:
Month By Month
Predictions

JANUARY

A wise man learns by the mistakes of others;
a fool by his own.

—Latin proverb

Highlights of the month

January is an important month because it sets the trend for the rest of the year. Much of your focus will be on work but while this is happening you will not be able to escape the power of Mars being in your zone of family and domestic affairs. This will continue for several months so it's better to deal with problems and challenges associated with close family members as and when they arise, before they get out of hand.

Between the 3rd and 5th your mood will be intense and passionate. You could be attracted to someone older or in authority. This may relate to your work because success, ambition, and power are playing a greater role in your life. Spend some quality time planning your projects because they are going to become central to your standard of living.

You will receive some acknowledgment for your meticulous skills and abilities sometime around the 10th. You will be able to combine work with pleasure so I suggest you enjoy your career and savour its rewards. You will find yourself in the public eye and your superiors will be particularly satisfied with your work. Job satisfaction will be very high on your agenda but remember that responsibility goes along with that.

Your life could be turned around by meeting someone very unusual around the 13th. Their perspective on life will totally alter your existing beliefs, but this will not be a bad thing if you remain open to the power of change. A solar eclipse on the 15th also highlights this fact and you will discover a lot more about yourself and how to deal with your closest relationships in every department of your life because of this.

After the 17th, when Jupiter enters the sign of Pisces, expect a more philosophical frame of mind to emerge. You will have a greater sensitivity to the requirements of others and an understanding of the principles of karma (the law of cause and effect). Your spiritual growth will be accelerated at this time.

Between the 20th and the 22nd involvement with new groups of people will enhance your sense of self and your life purpose as well. Friendships which involve group activities will become a greater focus in your life. You will begin to see the value of friend-ships and co-operation will become easier for you, both socially and within your family.

You will opt for a more personal style of relating after the 25th and up until the 27th an exciting phase of life can be expected where communication and a more active involvement on a one-to-one level should be anticipated. In your romantic affairs your interaction will be more animated.

Romance and friendship

You'll have to determine which of several appoint-ments you're going to prioritise around the 2nd. Your social objectives will be bothering and you may not feel as popular as you would like.

On the 5th, if you're not doing what you feel is enhancing your credibility, you could lose face. All you can do is your best and then leave the rest to providence.

New friends could be more of a worry than a support on the 7th. They will dump their problems at your door. What will you do under these circum-stances? Sit there and grin and bear it or waste hours with one who's not going to listen, anyway?

By the 9th you'll probably cut them off and it's quite likely you'll find the appropriate balance to deal with the situation.

Between the 11th and the 13th the Sun and Venus bring you large doses of charm and magnetic power. You could meet someone at this time who will give you the opportunity and confidence to attract more friends, and professional opportunities as well.

Between the 16th and the 18th, quick wit will be the order of the day, but you may also get yourself into a spot of bother. You mustn't try to outshine others.

On the 22nd and the 23rd you may be trying to make feeble excuses for not turning up to an engage-ment. Perhaps your diary is overloaded (or are you just being too apathetic?). Be a little more aware of what others are going to feel if you let them down, particularly if it's at the last minute.

Between the 28th and the 30th communication will centre upon another person's misunderstanding of your actions or words. They feel you have done something wrong by them, but you'll soon clear this up and the month can finish on a good note.

Work and money

Getting out and about, shopping and generally spending way too much money is on the cards between the 6th and the 10th. This will give you an opportunity to clear your mind, but you may not have any particular destination or financial strategy at this point so be careful that you don't end up with an empty wallet.

You'll complete a cycle of financial turmoil after the 17th and by the 19th will feel much more confi-dent that you have things under control. This is also a time of greater communication.

Secure a good deal for yourself at work between the 20th and the 22nd. This is a period of financial and professional growth and your interactions will be much sharper. There will be a renewed interest in human psychology, which will play an important role in your professional life after this.

Do not sweep work matters under the rug between the 25th and the 29th. You may think that these are inconsequential but that will be a mistake. Cutting corners will be out of the question. Pay more attention to detail and by doing so, greater success will be forthcoming in the coming weeks.

Destiny dates

Positive: 3, 4, 5, 11, 12, 13, 15, 16, 17, 18, 19, 20, 21

Negative: 2, 5, 7, 9

Mixed: 6, 7, 8, 10, 22, 23, 25, 26, 27, 28, 29, 30

Highlights of the month

You can take stock of your life throughout February and after the 2nd you will benefit from taking a look at yourself and spending some time away from the external world.

Playing out your martyr complex with friends is not the best plan of attack on the 7th as you may find yourself ensnared in a complex situation that is out of your control, anyhow. Render help where you can but don't become bogged down in endless problems that others want you to clean up.

New beginnings in your romantic life are heralded this month, especially between the 8th and the 11th. You will have a deep yearning for some soul-stirring friendship or love affair but you must be careful that this connection is not based upon pity or an inclination to see people through rose-coloured glasses when in fact they are just ordinary, down-to-earth people.

Around the 15th you may choose some new beginnings and daring moves on the home front. But this may create waves with loved ones who are more than happy to stay with the tried and tested rather than venture out into uncharted territory. You will have your work cut out for you in making these changes; but if you're sympathetic to their fear of change, slowly but surely you may be able to bring them around to your way of thinking. It pays to be careful about how you say things as much as what it is you have to say.

You will come under considerable pressure after the 18th and keeping the harmony between yourself and others will be one of the big challenges this month, especially if someone is pushing your buttons. You must use this time to keep calm and not react to each and every event around you.

You're particularly attractive between the 20th and the 22nd, so make sure you have plenty of space available in your diary to accommodate several exciting engagements. This is also a perfect time to persuade your partner gently to improve their social skills with you. If you're in a long-term committed partnership, it's an ideal way to re-establish your connection with each other.

Between the 23rd and the 28th could be a great time for resolving longstanding issues with friends or ex-partners. Making peace rather than war seems to be the catchcry for the last few days of February. And when the Sun joins Jupiter in your zone of friendships, a truce can finally be reached.

Romance and friendship

You'll feel great about yourself between the 2nd and the 7th, sweeping aside any aggression others may be placing in your way. You'll be methodical in dealing with personal reactions and won't understand why you feel so good when they're trying to bother you. You're getting on top of life.

You're brilliant in your discussions around the 8th and 9th and others may or may not agree with you but they will have to admit that your opinions are certainly interesting. One thing, however: it's best to stay away from politics and religion if you see an argument coming on!

Around the 12th your work situation will demand changes to plans, so get a clear overview before sharing what's going on with others. You don't want to come out having egg on your face.

After the 13th, you could feel yourself trapped in an emotional arrangement over which you have no control. Before committing yourself to giving someone a helping hand, it's best to analyse the situation and whether or not you have the resources to help them.

Between the 21st and the 23rd your personal charm will be striking hot, so you should be capable of attaining your romantic goals during this interval. If you're fortunate enough to come in touch with a newcomer on the scene, you could be like a dog with a bone thinking about them and this will cause you to be less productive than normal.

By the 25th you can resolve issues with someone whom you earlier fell out of favour with. Emotions may run high, so try to keep a lid on yours. You may be apprehensive about giving away too much by letting others know exactly how you feel.

Try to be level-headed, especially on the 28th when domestic discussions can also get out of hand. This is all about how you'll feel much better by maintaining control over your mind and your feelings.

Work and money

Between the 2nd and the 7th, a person may show you an unpleasant side of their nature. Making any hasty assessments of others will set you up for a fall, especially if you made them out to be a superhero. Rest assured that at some point even the most capable person will prove to be only human after all. It's all about accepting the good as well as the bad to foster better workplace relations.

Between the 8th and the 12th you'll be far more intense about money and you'll therefore attract less of it. This is one of the main principles of life and karma, remember that. Loving what you do and being content with your situation will go a lot further in bringing you the rewards you desire.

You could be short on patience around the 16th, especially if your pay has been held up. A renegotiation may be essential, particularly around the 21st.

Between the 25th and the 27th your negotiations could run into a snag because you could be too opinionated. You only lose others in your bid to convince them that you're right, even if you are.

Destiny dates

Positive: 15, 20, 21, 22, 23, 24
Negative: 3, 4, 5, 6, 13, 18
Mixed: 2, 7, 8, 9, 10, 11, 12, 25, 26, 27, 28

Highlights of the month

Put your thinking cap on between the 1st and the 5th because Mercury will stimulate your communication such as letter writing and public relations skills. You should find this period a tranquil few days with most things going to plan. Don't postpone important letters or e-mails at this time to get the response you need from people who are usually rather difficult to deal with.

Expect an avalanche of events, demands, social activities and communication between the 7th and the 11th. Mostly much of what happens during these few days will result in good news. Your career plans get the support and encouragement you require from the right people. Also, some of your life's challenges will be tackled in a much more confident manner, so you should easily find some novel solutions.

Deception in love and friendship could be part and parcel of the cycle between the 14th and the

16th. What you may discover could shock you or at the least make you less trusting of others. Incidentally, this may not necessarily relate specifically to your own relationship, but you may witness something about someone else that will cause you to question the very nature of relationships. This may happen around the 17th.

Your values will be changing during the month of March and you could therefore find yourself at odds with your own best interests. It will be hard to come to terms with some aspects of tradition or someone who holds very different opinions from your own.

Leading up to the 20th, you might very well decide to step away from a particular peer group that has been part of your life for sometime. Embrace these changes as part of your development and expect bigger and better things to open up as a result of your making better emotional and mental space in your world.

From the 21st till the 24th there is a positive influence from the planet Jupiter to your career zone. Your no-nonsense vision and down-to-earth approach will be a high-water mark for your professional direction, and it's likely others will easily distinguish your contributions, even if you're not working outside your home but are perhaps a homemaker. At the same time, a change of direction is in order, finding you in a gradual curve towards more inwardness.

On the 22nd, you need to be very clear-headed. Your thoughts and communications may not be quite in line with those of others and you could be misunderstood. Although this may seem harmless at the time, you'll be surprised at just what sort of repercussions can arise through poor communication.

Around the 25th, long-distance discussions will have a bearing on your life. If you are a parent of a child who is travelling or have a close relative who lives at a distance, there will be much more interaction with them via the telephone or the Internet.

Romance and friendship

Don't postpone important communications, especially in the first couple of days of the month. Between the 1st and the 5th you have the opportunity to set right any misunderstandings and, if need be, travelling to sort out these issues is advisable.

Your spouse, lover or best friend will be entering a period of tremendous frustration between the 5th and the 8th. You mustn't, however, buy into their victim mentality, because rest assured there will be plenty of it. Try to remind them that the negative periods of life are only temporary and things will improve.

On the 10th and the 11th you'll experience a greater level of social demands. If you have been unhappy with your personal situation, you're likely to push yourself towards an excessive lifestyle that could be self-destructive. Learn from your mistakes, but don't punish yourself.

By the 16th you'll be asking yourself many questions about life and love, especially if you find history repeating itself. To start, think carefully about how to deal with the recurrence of a situation or an event that you didn't handle so well in the past. It may be easy 'to fly off the handle', particularly around the 21st.

You can raise the benchmark in your love life and your friendships during the period of the 23rd to the 25th. Even if you feel as though you have fallen on desperate times you'll rediscover the secret of attracting a better quality of love into your life.

You'll have to expand your circle of power and between the 27th and the 30th it's likely you have a strong desire to do so but may suddenly be restricted through family circumstances. Once you start to enjoy more personal influence, you'll realise that disciplining your mind and your body become even more important.

Work and money

Between the 2nd and the 4th, get-rich-quick schemes may be attractive but remember you'll rarely get wealthy using these techniques. There are opportunities for you to enhance your financial status by the 6th. You'll become aware of opportunities.

If you have been stuck in a certain way of doing things, the universe may open the doors to you around the 11th and you'll find that your attraction and ability to take hold of the moment will be the foundation of success.

As yo...
16th, it w...
going to ...
direction, o...
feet on both...
going to bur...
greatest waste...

Around the 2...
don't believe yo...
they will be proje...

Between the 27...
control over what o...   ...o or
how they perceive yo...   ...e all of this
too personally.

Destiny dates

Positive: 1, 2, 3, 4, 21, 22, 23, 24
Negative: 8, 9, 10, 14, 15, 16, 17, 20
Mixed: 5, 6, 7, 11, 25, 27, 28, 29, 30

Highlights of the month

The name of the game in April is to make great first impressions and to put your best foot forward as you commence a new cycle, for it will add value to your life in terms of your self-esteem and your financial gains. You're idealistic and, on the 1st, 2nd and 3rd, you will be in a position to sway the opinions of others to your own advantage.

You will also be very interested in artistic pursuits and will find yourself in the company of others who have aesthetic interests and perhaps are more creative than your usual group of friends. This can be inspiring and stimulating, especially around the 5th when you will see life's possibilities in a new light. However, with Saturn entering your zone of creativity and romance, during its retrograde motion, you might feel like a fish out of water if you haven't been involved in these kinds of activities before.

Educational pursuits are very much highlighted

during the month of April, and taking on a new class, home study course or simply attending lectures with a view to improving yourself would be a good idea.

You might find yourself overly concerned by a loved one or youngster this month. Perhaps they are not handling practical day-to-day issues well and you'll be called in to make life easier for them. This could come to a head around the 15th.

You may also find yourself at odds with someone in a position of authority, so making business decisions may not be all that easy, especially if this person measures every step you try to make. If the pressure gets too much, sometime around the 18th, you may creatively decide to make some changes or even leave your work completely. You could be at a crossroad, professionally speaking.

After the 20th your personality is far more dynamic and outgoing than usual and you can use this to foster better relations on the work front with co-workers. There could be some competitiveness about your job at this time, so using your charm will help smooth over any tensions in the workplace.

Your ideals in love might be in for an overhaul around the 23rd when you comprehend that no one is perfect and that you must either adjust to the human frailties of the situation or get out of it altogether.

You're determined to achieve something of value this month, and the combination of Venus, the Sun and Pluto will cause you to achieve great things in spite of yourself. Money will be very important, but don't make this the be-all and end-all of life. Try to see beyond the material value of things.

Romance and friendship

Between the 1st and the 4th you have a very strong desire to enter into a new partnership but may find that too many forces are opposed to this happening.

Between the 11th and the 14th don't forget that friends are only human. Your expectation of them may be out of proportion to what is possible. On another front, you could be let down by false promises and also left in a position of having to organise the details of an outing when someone had previously agreed to do the job.

From the 16th till the 18th you'll be a great support to someone younger who has less experience than you. You'll be able to connect with their difficulties and you'll help them lift the burden from their shoulders by showing them the way. You mustn't underestimate the power you have in helping people out of a dark phase of their lives during April.

On the 24th your emotions are likely to be quite volatile but that will work to your advantage when you kiss and make up with your loved one.

Try not to hold on to grudges on the 26th and set aside valuable time to complete the task of sorting out your differences. If you both put your heads together and spend time planning more carefully, your relationship will feel much better for you.

Between the 28th and the 30th you mustn't let money become a point of contention in your relationship. If you can see that your partner or spouse is not handling money in the way that you would like, it's important to raise this issue and discuss it logically.

Work and money

You'll be worrying about the small change, which will cause you to lose sight of the value of the bigger picture. Around the 3rd and 4th, focus on bigger and better things and don't get petty over money.

On the 5th and 6th you'll have the opportunity to practise the art of large-heartedness and be prepared to share what you have without fear of loss.

Even if you're feeling low on energy on the 9th, you don't have to write off the day completely. Your enthusiasm can still muster assistance from others to help you get the job done.

On the 12th someone who doesn't really care about how you feel will drain you. They may be using you to achieve their own ends, so cut them out and don't pay attention to them anymore. Don't be used.

From the 18th till the 22nd make a last-minute dash to the finishing line if work hasn't been completed. Set aside time to complete these tasks, which should be better managed over the coming weeks.

Fortunately, by the 26th you'll have a better grasp of things and will be ready to deploy a new plan. Execute your schedule without delay.

You'll love your work on the 29th, but may have to deal with someone who's envious of your achievements. It's better to continue doing what you do best alone and not share too much of that with others. Disregard rumours on the 30th.

Destiny dates

Positive: 1, 2, 3, 4, 5, 16, 17, 19, 20, 21, 22, 26
Negative: 11, 12, 13, 14, 15, 23, 24, 26, 28, 30
Mixed: 18, 29

Highlights of the month

Your vision of life and what you think is possible may not be received too warmly by others, but this is an excellent time to make your dreams come true and not be fazed by others' negative opinions.

On the 3rd, when Mercury and Pluto create a favourable circumstance for you, you can make your dreams a reality. Excellence will help you ferret out some new opportunity, which will pave the way for a bright new future.

The Sun also produces excellent results for you around the 4th with a new job or promotional opportunity resulting in extra cash. As I said earlier, you mustn't let money blind you to other aspects of the situation. You may be more satisfied in a job which pays less money but certainly provides you with a greater degree of flexibility, creativity and workplace satisfaction due to the type of people you work with.

You could hit some extreme notes in the song of your life between the 15th and the 18th. You must figure out when enough is enough and not push your body or your emotions to the limits. Trying to keep up with friends, staying up late, eating and drinking too much, will result in negative mental and emotional states.

On the 19th writing things in style will help you to win a few Brownie points. If you're in a sales position or working in some type of industry that requires you to make a strong impact on others, this will be an excellent time to put your best foot forward and secure a deal.

If you're seeking to woo your love, this is benefited by your being able to write clearly and to some extent romantically. Don't be afraid to express a little nostalgia and sentimentality in your correspondence.

You want to be unique at this time and so you mustn't be afraid to step out of your normal comfort zone and do things, even if you feel uncomfortable initially. Spending some time alone can be the perfect way to help you appreciate your own uniqueness and this is what will make you stand out.

From the 28th till the 31st spiritual energies will dominate your life, so try to cultivate as many unusual or far-reaching ideas as possible. This is the start of great things, so don't let fear cheat you out of a better destiny.

Romance and friendship

Events move at an unexpected pace between the 3rd and the 8th. You will be caught off guard if you're not prepared. Around the 3rd, however, a certain person will help you become aware of an opportunity to which previously you were blind.

Read between the lines on the 8th if you want to understand clearly the feelings of someone you love. Don't let miscommunication create problems. It's best to do the talking rather than relying on a third party to deliver your messages.

On the 9th and the 10th you have a high level of magnetic power, and it's up to you to use it in whatever way you wish. People are going to judge your impeccable behaviour, so if your philosophy is one of 'do as I say, not as I do', be careful. Remain above reproach because your boss will be watching you closely.

You could be restless around the 17th and impulsively want to do something, but you could later regret it. One or two of your friends will perhaps be advising you differently on how to handle a particular situation and, although you'll see the merit of what both of them have to say, you'll definitely feel torn between the two sets of advice.

If, around the 23rd you feel as if you're in a relationship that is not quite satisfying for you, it might lead you to seek more exciting partners—someone you might consider more fulfilling.

Between the 28th till the 30th you'll find that

your level of awareness is superseding that of your friends', and you'll be ready to step out and try new things. If you have been feeling isolated, don't feel obliged to stay in the one place just to please them. Your peer group will have become a crutch for you.

Work and money

You have excellent opportunities professionally from the 5th but will also find yourself taking on an assignment that is bigger than you had anticipated. A commitment in sticking to your guns will certainly be difficult but will reward you handsomely if you don't collapse under the pressure around the 9th.

You need to find ways to minimise tension over the period of the 11th to the 14th and this could be a cycle in which you have to make social sacrifices for your own work. You'll feel good about this.

On the 22nd exercise patience and present your case without ambiguity. Even if changes occur you'll be in a better position to handle the outcome. Remember, you cannot control everything, so grin and bear it with patience.

On the 24th and the 25th you'll need quiet time to reflect upon the previous week and its impact upon your work strategies. This will be a good policy, especially if you need a comeback for someone who has done you wrong. Someone will say or do something that confuses you, and the way forward will not be all that clear until the 29th.

Destiny dates

Positive: 3, 4, 5, 6, 7, 10, 19, 28, 29, 30, 31
Negative: 11, 12, 13, 14, 15, 16, 17, 18
Mixed: 8, 9, 22, 24, 25

Highlights of the month

Don't force things in June. Try to be accommodating of other people's ideas because flexibility will be the best way for you to achieve what you want. Around the 4th, when Mars and Neptune oppose each other, you could be confused and finding it difficult to make head or tail of a situation. The secret at this time will be to understand clearly what you want and not rely on others to superimpose their views upon you.

On the 7th you'll find yourself once again in an imaginative yet competitive phase. You'll be seeking appreciation and admiration for who you are and what you're doing. If you don't quite receive this from your partner, spouse or other significant people in your life, you might end up demanding more than they are able to give you. I repeat, don't push too hard.

You'll want to have much more financial savvy, and a practical approach to your finances is the way to achieve this. Take as much time as you need to consult with those who are experts in this field and don't cut corners because you think it will cost you too much money to do so. Make an appointment with your accountant or a financial adviser around the 10th and remember, as the old saying goes, you need to spend money to make money.

Your drive and physical energy are extremely forceful and dominant when Mars influences your Sun sign after the 13th. I hope you have planned adequate exercise and acceptable outlets to redirect some of this power. It is at this juncture in your life that relationships can be made or broken due to the way you express yourself. Although you're right on several points, the way you express your opinions will make a big difference in terms of whether or not you're accepted. Plenty of physical exercise and of course a greater focus on your diet are essential during this phase of the year.

Between the 14th and the 20th your home life will come to the fore. Spending quality time with your relatives, redecorating your home and generally feeling more grounded and homebound will be spotlighted. You will definitely appreciate your past history much more and you may even find yourself discovering something very interesting about your early family life. Some of you may decide to begin your family tree and rummage through your old photographs to put together the pieces of your past.

When the Sun enters the third zone of travel you'll be physically active and on the go. From the

23rd till the 30th you'll be extremely busy and will probably have very little time, not only for those you love, but for yourself, too. Actually, if you look at your agenda, much of what you have on the top of the list is not as important as you think. Prioritising will definitely help lessen your tension.

Romance and friendship

You feel particularly idealistic about relationships this month. Between the 1st and the 7th you might end up convincing yourself that someone is worthy of you. Later you'll realise that you have been dealing with a person who's simply wasting your time and taking your good nature for granted.

Fortunately between the 15th and the 18th you won't be relying on accessories to make you feel better about yourself. This is a strong phase of romance, with Venus producing excellent results based upon who you are as a person not your fashion accessories. You can hold your head high and expect flattery and fine words from friends and strangers alike.

On the 20th, rendering good service selflessly will make you feel good and draw you closer to a friend. Health issues of a relative will require you to advise them and to share your wisdom to assist them in getting better.

You know exactly what you must do on the 22nd to improve your relationship but will have to consider your partner's sensitivities. You have to explain that the quickest way between emotional points A and B is a straight line.

Cold calculation is necessary on the 26th. If you feel that your love life is less than desirable, be more rational rather than emotional. This is a better game plan for you rather than ranting and raving and demanding that your emotional needs be met.

You could have great ideas related to travel or higher education around the 28th and will find yourself in the company of like-minded friends who want to share the experience with you.

Work and money

The month kicks off with excellent brainstorming and between the 1st and the 5th you'll find your workplace and your work partners invigorating. This will take the edge off your humdrum life and draw you to new educational prospects. Take a close look at the curriculum, though.

On the 7th you'll take time out to tackle other responsibilities rather than throwing yourself holus-bolus into your work.

You have a great sense of self-confidence between the 8th and the 13th and, if you're not happy with your work, approach your employer and change the terms you work under. The worst that can happen is that you'll get a refusal but in the process you'll gain extra respect by having the courage to speak up and express what you feel you're worth.

A friend's success on the 18th will be great

news. Your heart will be warmed and you'll also be inspired to do better in your work as well.

From the 20th till the 25th your intense moods need to be channelled into constructive projects, otherwise you'll fritter away valuable time and resources.

Destiny dates

Positive: 1, 2, 3, 4, 5, 6, 8, 9, 10, 11, 12, 13, 14, 15, 16, 17, 18, 19

Negative: Nil

Mixed: 7, 20, 21, 22, 23, 24, 25, 26, 27, 28, 29, 30

JULY

Highlights of the month

You have probably postponed an important discussion with an employer or other authority figure for sometime. That may be unavoidable now, especially around the 2nd. As long as you're prepared and can communicate your ideas properly with sufficient facts to back up your point of view, why should you worry? If you ask a question, you can only get a 'yes' or a 'no'. Even if the initial response is unfavourable, you will come out on top and furthermore you will gain the respect of your boss by speaking out.

If there are longstanding issues with a sibling or close neighbour, there's no use in burying your head in the sand. Between the 5th and the 9th, why not invite dialogue for a peace treaty so that harmony can once again be restored in your relationship?

After the 10th, when Venus enters your zone of romance, expect a love affair to either flare up again or someone new to enter into your life. You mustn't let awkwardness hinder such a great opportunity.

Playing shy or hard to get may also be a problem because this could ruin a perfectly good chance for love and sexual satisfaction.

Venus also promises you fantastic responses in any job interviews you may attend. Favourable planetary circumstances abound between the 13th and the 20th, so you should make yourself available and don't be afraid to make yourself look even more admirable than usual. A new hair colour or pair of shoes that make a statement about who you are will contribute to your success and make a great impact on your interviewers.

You will take a greater interest in a more disciplined approach to work, health and life's other important daily routines towards the close of the month as Saturn re-enters your sixth zone of work and dietary practices around the 21st. If you have developed some bad habits, personal or otherwise, this will be the time when you say: 'This is a turning point. I must turn over a new leaf!'

On or about the 25th you will place a greater emphasis on your emotional security and will also be analysing whether or not those in your life have been providing you with that special form of nourishment.

Real estate will also come to the fore and there is a strong possibility of either purchasing or selling a house or land at this time. If you're not necessarily a property owner, this will be the time that a makeover or renovation is likely to be a bigger part of your life's goals.

Romance and friendship

Between the 1st and the 3rd a romance that has waned will be resurrected; but on the 4th, be careful because, even though your affections will be getting stronger by the day, something will abruptly change your opinion. Fortunately others will encourage you and things should settle down by the 6th.

Put aside your mistrust of a friend who genuinely wishes to assist you on the 7th. They certainly do have your best interests at heart, so don't miss the opportunity to improve yourself through their advice.

It will be difficult to balance or to juggle your complex social calendar around the 11th. It's not easy, but it's possible. There will be excellent opportunities not only for social interaction but also for deep and meaningful romance. This powerful energy should increase up till about the 15th or 16th.

You can expect an encounter or two around the 18th that could also include considerable humour and creative endeavours. You will have to ditch a family event on the 19th to make way for additional invitations.

Transforming your relationships will be a challenge between the 24th and the 26th, especially if you feel that the situation is becoming one-sided. Your partner needs to see the real benefits of change. If they're stubborn or stuck in their old ways this will a monumental task for you.

For singles the period of the 27th to the 29th

indicates you'll have to be daring if you want any sort of romantic or relationship success. The planets favour you taking a step in the direction of your destiny. Courage will be the essential factor and you must not look backwards.

On the 30th you'll have doubts about a new partnership, but what are you going to do? Nothing stands still and neither can you. Be confident that your decision will bring you a better life.

Work and money

On the 2nd your mind will be concerned, if not worried or perhaps angry, over a financial matter that you cannot quite resolve. Tire yourself out because going to bed early will only see you going over and over the numbers without any final resolutions and very little sleep.

If you're not clear on a legal matter or accounting procedures on the 5th, why waste good thought power on it? Get expert help.

You'll be prioritising your expenditure around the 9th to the 17th. This is because your bills will be mounting up on your desk. But not everything has to be done immediately, so try to figure out a way to stagger your payments so that this doesn't impact upon your social life or family commitments.

You might think you're wasting your time listening to a friend's suggestion regarding a career change between the 18th and the 20th, but don't be so hasty. Not only will they offer you great advice but they will even have several terrific connections to help you secure the position you're looking for.

Pull out your little black book on the 22nd because you will have overlooked the fact that an acquaintance is able to introduce you to a third party or advisor who could further assist you in your career goal objectives.

Destiny dates

Positive: 1, 2, 3, 6, 7, 8, 10, 18, 20, 22, 25, 27, 28, 29
Negative: 12, 21, 30
Mixed: 2, 5, 9, 10, 11, 13, 14, 15, 16, 17, 19

Highlights of the month

Taking a gamble throughout August may seem like the best possible move, but is it really? With the planets Jupiter, Mars, Saturn and Uranus all battling it out for supremacy over the control of your attitudes and decisions, you may throw all cares to the wind only to regret it later.

Between the 3rd and the 6th you may be surprised by the behaviour of a friend who chooses to do something completely out of the ordinary. You may not know how to act as a consequence.

Around this time you may also be wasteful and overconfident. Try to be more appreciative of what you have. It's imperative that you develop a feeling of gratitude and look at the positive things in your life rather than peering over the fence hoping to keep up with the Jones's.

A loved one suffers some health issues between the 7th and the 10th, so you need to be there for them. This may even require you to take some time off work so that you can be available to help them. If you have been feeling cool or aloof in your romantic responses to this person, the weird and wonderful thing about these planetary transits is that they may draw you closer to each other.

A sudden exit by a long-term friend could leave you reeling around the 15th. You must understand that the nature of friendships is such that time does change people and their circumstances must also reflect this. This is not necessarily an end to friendship but a readjustment.

You may be involved in helping someone move back, re-establish or relocate their lives. If it is someone who is related to you, this could be an emotionally cathartic time and one that produces some important spiritual developments in your life.

You can express yourself in a really wonderful way by the 23rd but you may mistrust your own feelings due to the really unsavoury combination of Mars and Saturn. During this minor cycle you may be throwing yourself into work simply to avoid the inevitable showdown with someone you love.

Stop sweeping your feelings under the rug because talking about how you feel will have a magical tonic effect on your love life. You'll be so surprised at the response you receive from transparency and straightforwardness.

Between the 21st and the 31st irresistible forces come into contact with immovable objects, so to speak. A period of compromise is absolutely essential for you to bring all the pieces of your life together, especially in your marriage or love life. As a Taurean, flexibility is one of your major life lessons and it will be highlighted at this juncture.

Romance and friendship

Be prepared to give much more than you receive on the 2nd and be careful this doesn't impact on your health. Become more educated about the way people are. Your enthusiasm could cause you to take more of a gamble than you should.

Diet, health and other important issues relating to your physical wellbeing will be spotlighted between the 3rd and the 6th. You must not make excuses as to why time is a dominant factor that disallows you to get this part of your life right. An excuse is an excuse, but where there is a will there is a way, remember that.

You can take full advantage of the playful and demonstrative responses of your partner or a new lover between the 11th and the 15th. What you receive from them will please you and you'll both want to share love and life to get your romance moving in the right direction. For those of you who are not particularly connected romantically this is an excellent time to strike up a friendship with someone who's genuine.

You have got to stop wondering what it's like to travel to a destination that you have been dreaming about. From the 19th to the 23rd, act upon your dreams and do work towards that. This will also relate to the fact that a person you love has decided to leave the scene and you have the chance to connect with him or her in a distant place.

On the 29th you recognise that you cannot always control the forces around you. Your personal life could feel as if it's out of your reach and, rather than swimming against the current, you should go with the flow.

Work and money

You could be short-changed and anxious due to financial circumstances changing between the 1st and the 4th. You'll be unable to do anything about it due to your previous agreement to hand over your power to someone else.

You know, it's never too late to ask questions and this is important because by the 13th you'll experience considerable frustration in your work and will feel trapped. It might sound like too much hard work but it's up to you to go the extra mile to sort out these issues.

A decision to move in a new direction after the 16th requires immense willpower on your part. The first stage of the game is usually full of excitement, but don't forget that after a while the reality of what is necessary to complete the task can make it seem rather daunting.

You have got what it takes to complete an educational programme between the 21st and the

25th. A round of discussions surrounding this will be useful because you will feel better. Hang in there; commit yourself to the task because it will all be worth it in the end.

Destiny dates

Positive: 11, 12, 14, 19, 20

Negative: 1, 2, 3, 4, 5, 6, 7, 8, 9, 10

Mixed: 13, 15, 16, 21, 22, 23, 24, 25, 26, 27, 28, 29, 30, 31

SEPTEMBER

Highlights of the month

This really is one of the best months in which to consider marriage and other significant relationships. Venus moving through your seventh zone of partnerships, marriage and important karmic relationships brings with it great prospects to seek out your best soulmate.

If you are already involved in a serious relationship, a new cycle of love commences in your life. Between the 1st and the 7th you may feel your heart missing a few beats because you're introduced to someone who fits your perfect mate profile.

This is also an excellent time to take pleasure in and be thankful for your association with friends and others who have been there to support you in the past. From the 9th, a new and important friendship will develop, or perhaps someone you have only casually been involved with could suddenly dazzle you and make you realise what you have overlooked in them up till now.

In trying to be too many things to too many people, you may inadvertently step on another's toes. When Mars enters your zone of close relationships on the 14th you may become possessive, demanding, and will expect too much from your partner. Nevertheless, this period of the month offers you a great deal of passionate interplay.

Similarly, if you're with someone who is of like-mind, this could be a very playful period and one in which you can further cement the bonds of friendship. The spirit of co-operation is very important for you to make the most of this sometimes aggressive planet.

Between the 19th and the 23rd, please take as many precautions as you can not to end up in hot water or create accidents or other physical mishaps. You will have a tendency to rush and make errors, so in your working life, check your work thoroughly and then check it again. It may also be a good idea to get someone else to go over your work so that a second pair of eyes can pick up those errors you might have missed.

You'll be taking your work very seriously after the 25th; in fact, you could tend to become a workaholic of sorts. You may run into a spot of bother if your work demands take you away from your personal responsibilities, especially if someone you love doesn't understand the dynamics of your professional commitments during this phase of your life.

The way you interact with your co-workers will need an overhaul. Developing a better rapport with others is a great way to improve your chance for success. While the Sun is transiting through your sixth zone of work after the 26th, try to make a greater effort at understanding other people's points of view.

Health issues are also again likely to take a higher priority after the 28th. Don't postpone those medical checkups, even if you have a slight apprehension about doing so. Dental work, booking into a new gym and researching ways in which you can turn back the ageing clock will be a part of your learning curve.

Romance and friendship

This is an important period of love for you. Between the 1st and the 7th you will more than likely meet someone and will hit it off immediately with them. You also re-establish a greater contact with some of your friends. If you have found communication waning, this is a period when things can get back on track.

Around the 9th, a casual affair or one-night stand might start to develop into something more than you had expected it to. This person may have been in the picture previously but you may not have paid all that much attention to them. Now things will be different.

Around the 10th your desires will be very strong and someone in your life will take on a much greater or special significance. You will feel attracted to each other and perhaps too much so. Your desires could even become obsessive.

Between the 15th and the 17th, issues of control will dominate your personal landscape. You will want to get what you want without concerns for your friends or partners. You also have a strong need to demonstrate that you're a worthwhile and successful individual, but trying too hard to prove this may only make it look quite the opposite. In a relaxed way, without saying too much, try to prove your worth by your deeds.

You will be more closely involved with another person who now may well become your highest priority. Marriage, contracts and partnerships are likely to be sources of happiness between the 24th and the 26th, and they have plenty of lessons to teach you.

After the 28th you will be the centre of attention because of some personal achievement that others may envy. Share this only with those whom you trust the most.

Work and money

You'll be poring over your accounts and trying to become more financially responsible between the 6th and the 10th. You'll have some interesting ideas that could give you a breakthrough in ways to save money and cut back costs.

You should be able to work with others in a productive manner from the 12th to the 14th. If you have been having difficulty with an employer, you'll find it much easier to get on with them and will feel as if they have finally accepted you for who you are rather than wanting you to be someone else.

Your financial involvement with other people is highlighted between the 16th and the 20th. This may or may not make you feel good, depending on the level of independence you're able to exert in the relationship. Business people with independent concerns could find themselves hamstrung by a partner or agent who is not towing the line.

Investments are definitely your focus between the 23rd and the 25th. Keep yourself clear and uncluttered by worries or extraneous activities that could cause you to be cloudy in your judgement.

Destiny dates

Positive: 1, 2, 3, 4, 5, 6, 7, 8, 9, 10, 12, 13, 14, 24, 26
Negative: 15, 21, 22, 28
Mixed: 16, 17, 19, 20, 23, 25

Highlights of the month

It's a well-known astrological fact that when the Sun combines with Saturn it can be a rather trying time due to the heavy workload and additional responsibilities that may be coming at you from many different directions.

From the 1st, you will feel an increase in the number of duties expected of you. Hopefully in the previous month you have organised your diary and list of priorities so that what is thrown at you now is not going to overwhelm you and cause you to make mistakes and, worse still, wear you out.

The influence of Mars on your Sun sign in the first week of October is a saving grace and will give you ample physical energy to work long and hard. Keep up your exercise regime as this will give you energy rather than diminish it. Between the 3rd and the 5th you're going to need an extra dose of power to handle the rather long working days because it seems as if this will be a very productive period, indeed.

It's very important to recognise your own goodness and strengths. Around the 18th, when Venus enters into a favourable relationship with the Sun, you will feel aware of what you can and can't do. There's also an opportunity for you to connect with older friends who are wiser and who can advise you on strengthening your talents and achieving more in life. Take heed of what they advise.

A business partnership is not a bad idea after the 23rd. If someone has been prodding you to do something independently, remember you don't necessarily have to 'jump out of the pan into the fire'. Give them a fair hearing because, of course, they are flattering you by asking you to be involved. You can offer your services part-time to see whether or not this has the makings of a successful venture.

Be prepared for challenges from those who may be a little envious of the power that you exude after the 25th. You will find yourself in opposition because of the way you come across. Someone could question your values or reason for doing things. You probably won't appear to them as you'd like to but sometimes this happens.

On the 28th Mars enters your eighth zone of joint finances and other shared resources. Power or issues of control will be very much a problem that you need to get your head around. Apart from the taxation, financial and material concerns involved, some struggle surrounding sexual intimacy could also rear its head.

Romance and friendship

You'll be taking your work very seriously after the 2nd. In fact, you could tend to become a workaholic of sorts. You will run into a spot of bother if your work demands take you away from your personal relationships, especially if the one you love doesn't understand the dynamics of your professional commitments during this phase of your life.

Between the 3rd and the 5th someone may be attracted to you but they don't particularly fit the mould and your peers may ridicule you for wanting to get involved. But you would rather do it your way and will want to get rid of any preconditioned ideas about how you should behave. Cast aside all judgements and concerns about what others think. Your choices will make you secure and happy in the long-term, whether or not others accept you.

A show of strength is what is necessary around the 18th and you may need to stomp on someone just to prove the point. If you are in a position of responsibility—for example, looking after family or children—there are going to be a few days where you are going to have to make some distasteful decisions and quite likely upset others. But you know this will just have to be the case and that it could get worse before it gets better.

One good turn deserves another on the 20th. But make it one good turn, please, not ten! If you are playing the Good Samaritan and have been giving someone assistance, don't become the victim when they make unreasonable demands and expect you to go well beyond the call of duty. Someone you have been assisting will be playing you for a fool, and the onus is on you to be aware of the manipulative games they are playing.

Between the 28th and the 30th, Mars triggers your need to understand your shared resources. Working on being economical with natural resources will impact upon the respect someone has for you. Become more aware of the global impact of your behaviour. This will open up a whole new way of looking at things and you'll start to feel more comfortable in the way you approach energy and conservation.

Work and money

From the 3rd till the 9th you'll throw a huge amount of energy into your career decisions. You will appear commanding and assertive and are more likely to be respected for your work and input on different objects.

On or about the 11th someone may be hell-bent on roping you into a business idea that you don't feel comfortable about. Your commonsense tells you this is not something that will work. Trust your intuition on it.

Between the 17th and the 20th you can use your contacts to gain leverage. Don't be surprised to find yourself in the midst of an upper-class social group at an important party or function. You'll be surprised at how easily you fit in with them.

You have an eager interest in what makes things tick around the 23rd. You'll be curious about learning other aspects of your work and this will trigger an interest in pursuing another career.

Between the 20th and the 24th a new mental cycle commences. Research will be a very important component of your work over the coming weeks.

You'll want to investigate new strategies for how you can grow your nest egg between the 29th and the 31st. Financial agreements work smoothly to your advantage and your negotiations come to favourable conclusions.

Destiny dates

Positive: 1, 6, 7, 8, 9, 17, 18, 19, 20, 21, 22, 23, 24, 29, 30, 31

Negative: 2, 11, 25

Mixed: 3, 4, 5, 28

Highlights of the month

You may not come across the way you have expected during the period of the 1st till the 3rd. If you spend too much time worrying about what other people think, then you will definitely find yourself in a predicament where you neither satisfy yourself nor others. Just be yourself and try to feel as comfortable as you can.

It is an important time to re-configure and de-compress your most important relationships this month and, from the 4th till the 9th, you will be spending a good deal of time talking about how you feel and how you can improve those most dear relationships.

Around the 5th you will be called away to do work, which could intrude upon these discussions, and you must not be seen to be slacking off or losing interest. Re-assert your commitment at this time.

With the extraordinary aspect of Mercury to Jupiter, the timeline from the 6th till the 10th is also highly beneficial for you in advertising that you're working in a larger scale and increasing your circle of influence. Your popularity will grow and friendships should be numerous.

After the 15th you can really knuckle down and feel as though you're getting somewhere with your work and your finances. Long and determined application to the job at hand will ensure great results for you. Patience also seems to be one of your key words throughout this period.

Up until the 20th you might find that the going gets a little less easy. You will need to make some important changes as you will be entering a very new stage of life that could take a while to adjust to.

Between the 20th and the 23rd you will be confused about your role with others. Should you take the lead or follow? Don't let your self-consciousness overpower you. Show others what you are made of!

Between the 22nd and the 29th you have a greater interest in such things as spiritual regeneration, taxes, death and other types of physical and sexual healing. The concept of Tantra or the ancient wisdom of connecting with your inner self through such things as sexual intimacy will fascinate you. Tie up your tax and other financial obligations during this cycle.

The month finishes with Venus entering your seventh house, your zone of relationships on the

29th. You have tremendous expectations from your partner and likewise they are expecting you to 'step up to the plate' and do your part to promote as much harmony as possible between you. Generally this is an excellent cycle and one that gives you the edge socially and romantically.

Romance and friendship

Between the 1st and the 3rd be prepared to stand on your own two feet and offer your opinions fearlessly. A show of strength is necessary and this will clearly demonstrate to others how you feel about things. By being decisive you will also attract a better calibre of person into your life.

Work more closely with your loved ones so there are no crossed lines with respect to appointments and engagements that you may have double-booked. Between the 4th and the 9th you'll be spending a lot of time getting closer to those you love on the home front.

Unexpected work delays on the 5th might be misinterpreted as a lack of interest in your spouse or partner. Let them know you love them and this could be the perfect time to buy them an unannounced gift.

Luck is with you between the 4th and the 10th when Mercury and Jupiter bring you a dose of good fortune. This is an excellent period for you to expand your social circle of friends and have some carefree fun.

After the 15th you might not really want to talk about the problems that are affecting you and a loved one. But you know better than anyone else that sweeping the problem under the rug is only going to create a monster for you down the track. It's better to tackle this issue now and be done with it.

Between the 18th and the 20th discuss lifestyle changes with the one you love. Both of you may be on the same page in as much as you want to move from your current location and try something completely out of the ordinary. If this doesn't actually mean moving residence, a weekend away could be just what the doctor ordered.

A time of healing can be expected between the 24th and the 29th and spiritual growth will be spotlighted. The areas that need to be addressed are of a sexual nature. If you have been in a long-term relationship that has become a little stale, it could be time to spice it up. Of course, this takes commitment and an honest reappraisal of your own part in the process.

With Venus casting its favourable rays of love on your zone of marriage on the 29th you can look forward to a renewed and enthusiastic period of love and intimacy. Try not to be too demanding of your lover at this time, especially if you are both readjusting to some new emotional understanding between you. Patience will be necessary to explore the deeper aspects of your love.

Work and money

Between the 4th and the 10th you'll be feeling the pinch and won't quite know how to handle the new tasks delegated to you. If you let your fear dominate you, this will be a difficult time, indeed, so ask and ye shall receive.

From the 16th till the 20th, working on a new filing system or planning mechanism will be ideal to help you organise your work life and the many other appointments that are more than likely while the Sun is transiting through your sixth zone of work.

On the 18th and the 19th you will be dealing with someone who is as stubborn as yourself and this will be frustrating. You'll quickly realise that one of you is going to have to yield otherwise this could become a confrontational situation.

Between the 27th and the 30th, clearly communicate important information. The key to gaining support is to measure your speech and rephrase anything that might be in doubt by others. You'll hastily need to exit while giving key instructions to someone. Postpone important dialogue until you both have the time to focus and get it right.

Destiny dates

Positive: 15, 24, 25, 26
Negative: 1, 2, 3, 18, 19, 20, 21, 22, 23
Mixed: 4, 5, 6, 7, 8, 9, 10, 27, 28, 29, 30

Highlights of the month

You must continue to broaden your intellectual and educational horizons, as this will be your ticket to a bigger and brighter world throughout the coming years. Don't get lazy now, because opportunities to enhance your skill set are offered to you from the 1st of December.

Mars and Neptune create a fantastic energy for you in which you can make things happen. Dreams or airy-fairy concepts now become tangible and you will be able to promote your ideas to listening ears.

Speaking of education and study, around the 7th Mars also enters the same zone of educational pursuits, which gives an even greater priority to this aspect of your life. Some Taureans may become obsessively concerned with travel as well so this is a time to do what you can to set the wheels in motion on this particular aspect of your life.

Leading up to Christmas, you will be testing your

stamina and the limits of your capabilities, so try to pace yourself a little more evenly, especially around the 16th when the Sun and Jupiter cause you to promise more than you can deliver if many friends are demanding your assistance or time.

Excellent transits await you between the 15th and the 20th. Mercury, Venus and the Sun all provide you with ample opportunity to set up the festive season to mix friendship, business and family life into one big joyous bundle of fun.

You could again be in the limelight, especially with superiors, in relation to your work and may called upon to act as a catalyst for the smooth functioning of some Christmas events. Again don't overdo it and be prepared to accept your limits.

Travel could be on the cards after the 21st when the Sun enters the ninth house of journeys. You will have connections with people afar and your interest in different cultures and unusual characters will expand as well.

The final powerful influence of the year is Mars coming in contact with your career sector, indicating that you will finish 2010 with a huge burst of energy and this will impact favourably on your career decisions and your family life.

Romance and friendship

Get your books out because it is an intense period of learning for you in the last month of 2010. You can enhance your knowledge base by reading and investigating new avenues of self-improvement around the 1st. This will go a long way to helping you in your relationships.

Mars also stimulates your desire for knowledge around the 7th and you will be quite happy to spend some time reading quietly without the disturbance of friends, or even family members, for that matter. You could be curious about studying different cultures and travel will also be on your mind.

Build your energy reserves just before Christmas and don't take on too much, especially around the 16th. Jupiter in combination with the Sun will make you exaggerate certain things and possibly even cause you to overestimate your physical endurance. Expect heavy demands from everyone.

Between the 15th and the 20th you'll have a great time partying and mixing with many friends and family members. Mercury, Venus and the Sun are responsible for this and will also give you a taste of some youthful action by way of music, dance and other exciting events.

Arranging the Christmas party at the office may also fall on your shoulders so be prepared to dedicate time to making the event a fun-filled one for all concerned.

Christmas may be spent away this year and you might decide to travel sometime around the 21st just as the Sun passes through your zone of long-distance travel. You'll come in touch with some unusual people and will feel rather restless but still in a very good mood.

Family life will be very fulfilling in the last part of the year, with Mars continuing to offer you some excellent planetary vibrations.

Work and money

On the 5th you'll be able to make something wonderful happen professionally. If you have been determined to achieve a longstanding goal, a breakthrough can be realised through the help of a superior.

How you package your ideas will be your main focus on the 10th. An idea may be brilliant but if others are unimpressed by your presentation, an opportunity may fall by the wayside. Spend more time elaborating and building a story around your offering.

Sharing creative ideas with a close friend will result in some brilliant business strategies, but you mustn't rush headlong into the unknown between the 15th and the 20th. Listen to what's on offer and also point out any pitfalls you perceive. Make a show of strength and ensure the pros are outweighed by the cons.

Between the 18th and the 25th you'll be dealing with people whose minds change like the wind and this will be frustrating. No sooner have you given them a directive for a plan and they will have changed their course of action. You will need to prove your leadership abilities under these circumstances.

Destiny dates

Positive: 1, 5, 7, 10, 15, 16, 17, 18, 19, 20, 21
Negative: 24, 25, 26, 27, 28, 29, 30
Mixed: 22, 23 .

2010:
Astronumerology

Time is but the stream I go a-fishin' in.

—Henry David Thoreau

The power behind your name

By adding the numbers of your name you can see which planet is ruling you. Each of the letters of the alphabet is assigned a number, which is listed below. These numbers are ruled by the planets. This is according to the ancient Chaldean system of numerology and is very different to the Pythagorean system to which many refer.

Each number is assigned a planet:

AIQJY	=	1	Sun
BKR	=	2	Moon
CGLS	=	3	Jupiter
DMT	=	4	Uranus
EHNX	=	5	Mercury
UVW	=	6	Venus
OZ	=	7	Neptune
FP	=	8	Saturn
—	=	9	Mars

Notice that the number 9 is not aligned with a letter because it is considered special. Once the numbers have been added you will see that a single planet rules your name and personal affairs. Many famous actors, writers and musicians change their names to attract the energy of a luckier planet. You can experiment with the list and try new names or add the letters of your second name to see how that vibration suits you. It's a lot of fun!

Here is an example of how to find out the power of your name. If your name is John Smith, calculate the ruling planet by assigning each letter to a number in the table like this:

```
J O H N S M I T H
1 7 5 5  3 4 1 4 5
```

Now add the numbers like this:
$1 + 7 + 5 + 5 + 3 + 4 + 1 + 4 + 5 = 35$
Then add $3 + 5 = 8$

The ruling number of John Smith's name is 8, which is ruled by Saturn. Now study the name-number table to reveal the power of your name. The numbers 3 and 5 will also play a secondary role in John's character and destiny, so in this case you would also study the effects of Jupiter and Mercury.

Name-number table

Your name number	Ruling planet	Your name characteristics
1	**Sun**	Magnetic individual. Great energy and life force. Physically dynamic and sociable. Attracts good friends and individuals in powerful positions. Good government connections. Intelligent, impressive, flashy and victorious. A loyal number for relationships.
2	**Moon**	Soft, emotional nature. Changeable moods but psychic, intuitive senses. Imaginative nature and empathetic expression of feelings. Loves family, mother and home life. Night owl who probably needs more sleep. Success with the public and/or women.
3	**Jupiter**	Outgoing, optimistic number with lucky overtones. Attracts opportunities without trying. Good sense of timing. Religious or spiritual aspirations.

Your name number	Ruling planet	Your name characteristics
		Can investigate the meaning of life. Loves to travel and explore the world and people.
4	Uranus	Explosive character with many unusual aspects. Likes the untried and novel. Forward thinking, with many extraordinary friends. Gets fed up easily so needs plenty of invigorating experiences. Pioneering, technological and imaginative. Wilful and stubborn when wants to be. Unexpected events in life may be positive or negative.
5	Mercury	Quick-thinking mind with great powers of speech. Extremely vigorous life; always on the go and lives on nervous energy. Youthful attitude and never grows old. Looks younger than actual age. Young friends and humorous disposition. Loves reading and writing.
6	Venus	Delightful personality. Graceful and attractive character who cherishes friends

Your name number	Ruling planet	Your name characteristics
		and social life. Musical or artistic interests. Good for money making as well as abundant love affairs. Career in the public eye is possible. Loves family but is often overly concerned by friends.
7	**Neptune**	Intuitive, spiritual and self-sacrificing nature. Easily misled by those who need help. Loves to dream of life's possibilities. Has curative powers. Dreams are revealing and prophetic. Loves the water and will have many journeys in life. Spiritual aspirations dominate worldly desires.
8	**Saturn**	Hard-working, focused individual with slow but certain success. Incredible concentration and self-sacrifice for a goal.
		Money orientated but generous when trust is gained. Professional but may be a hard taskmaster. Demands

		highest standards and needs to learn to enjoy life a little more.
9	**Mars**	Fantastic physical drive and ambition. Sports and outdoor activities are keys to wellbeing. Confrontational. Likes to work and play just as hard. Caring and protective of family, friends and territory. Individual tastes in life but is also self-absorbed. Needs to listen to others' advice to gain greater success.

Your 2010 planetary ruler

Astrology and numerology are very intimately connected. As already shown, each planet rules over a number between 1 and 9. Both your name *and* your birth date are ruled by planetary energies.

Add the numbers of your birth date and the year in question to find out which planet will control the coming year for you.

For example, if you were born on the 12th of November, add the numerals 1 and 2 (12, your day of birth) and 1 and 1 (11, your month of birth) to the year in question, in this case 2010 (the current year), like this:

$1 + 2 + 1 + 1 + 2 + 0 + 1 + 0 = 8$

The planet ruling your individual karma for 2010 will be Saturn because this planet rules the number 8.

You can even take your ruling name-number as shown earlier and add it to the year in question to throw more light on your coming personal affairs, like this:

John Smith = 8

Year coming = 2010

8 + 2 + 0 + 1 + 0 = 11

1 + 1 = 2

Therefore, 2 is the ruling number of the combined name and date vibrations. Study the Moon's number 2 influence for 2010.

Outlines of the year number ruled by each planet are given below. Enjoy!

1 is the year of the Sun

Overview

The Sun is the brightest object in the heavens and rules number 1 and the sign of Leo. Because of this the coming year will bring you great success and popularity.

You'll be full of life and radiant vibrations and are more than ready to tackle your new nine-year cycle, which begins now. Any new projects you commence are likely to be successful.

Your health and vitality will be very strong and your stamina at its peak. Even if you happen to have the odd problem with your health, your recuperative power will be strong.

You have tremendous magnetism this year so social popularity won't be a problem for you. I see many new friends and lovers coming into your life. Expect loads of invitations to parties and fun-filled outings. Just don't take your health for granted as you're likely to burn the candle at both ends.

With success coming your way, don't let it go to your head. You must maintain humility, which will make you even more popular in the coming year.

Love and pleasure

This is an important cycle for renewing your love and connections with your family, particularly if you have children. The Sun is connected with the sign of Leo and therefore brings an increase in musical and theatrical activities. Entertainment and other creative hobbies will be high on your agenda and bring you a great sense of satisfaction.

Work

You won't have to make too much of an effort to be successful this year because the brightness of the Sun will draw opportunities to you. Changes in work are likely and, if you have been concerned that opportunities are few and far between, 2010 will be different. You can expect some sort of promotion or an increase in income because your employers will take special note of your skills and service orientation.

Improving your luck

Leo is the ruler of number 1 and, therefore, if you're born under this star sign, 2010 will be particularly lucky. For others, July and August, the months of Leo, will bring good fortune. The 1st, 8th, 15th and 22nd hours of Sundays especially will give you a unique sort of luck in any sort of competition or activities generally. Keep your eye out for those born under Leo as they may be able to contribute something to your life and may even have a karmic connection to you. This is a particularly important year for your destiny.

Your lucky numbers in this coming cycle are 1, 10, 19 and 28.

2 is the year of the Moon

Overview

There's nothing more soothing than the cool light of the full Moon on a clear night. The Moon is emotional and receptive and controls your destiny in 2010. If you're able to use the positive energies of the Moon, it will be a great year in which you can realign and improve your relationships, particularly with family members.

Making a commitment to becoming a better person and bringing your emotions under control will also dominate your thinking. Try not to let your emotions get the better of you throughout the coming year because you may be drawn into the changeable nature of these lunar vibrations as well. If you fail to keep control of your emotional life you'll later regret some of your actions. You must blend careful thinking with feeling to arrive at the best results. Your luck throughout 2010 will certainly be determined by the state of your mind.

Because the Moon and the sign of Cancer rule the number 2 there is a certain amount of change to be expected this year. Keep your feelings steady and don't let your heart rule your head.

Love and pleasure

Your primary concern in 2010 will be your home and family life. You'll be finally keen to take on those renovations, or work on your garden. You may even think of buying a new home. You can at last carry out some of those plans and make your dreams come true. If you find yourself a little more temperamental than usual, do some extra meditation and spend time alone until you sort this out. You mustn't withhold your feelings from your partner as this will only create frustration.

Work

During 2010 your focus will be primarily on feelings and family; however, this doesn't mean you can't make great strides in your work as well. The Moon rules the general public and what you might find is that special opportunities and connections with the world at large present themselves to you. You could be working with large numbers of people.

If you're looking for a better work opportunity, try to focus your attention on women who can give you a hand. Use your intuition as it will be finely tuned this year. Work and career success depends upon your instincts.

Improving your luck

The sign of Cancer is your ruler this year and because the Moon rules Mondays, both this day of the week and the month of July are extremely lucky for you. The 1st, 8th, 15th and 22nd hours on Mondays will be very powerful. Pay special attention to the new and full Moon days throughout 2010.

The numbers 2, 11 and 29 are lucky for you.

3 is the year of Jupiter

Overview

The year 2010 will be a number 3 year for you and, because of this, Jupiter and Sagittarius will dominate your affairs. This is extremely lucky and shows you'll be motivated to broaden your horizons, gain more money and become extremely popular in your social circles. It looks like 2010 will be a fun-filled year with much excitement.

Jupiter and Sagittarius are generous to a fault and so, likewise, your open-handedness will mark the year. You'll be friendly and helpful to all of those around you.

Pisces is also under the rulership of the number 3 and this brings out your spiritual and compassionate nature. You'll become a much better person, reducing your negative karma by increasing your self-awareness and spiritual feelings. You will want to share your luck with those you love.

Love and pleasure

Travel and seeking new adventures will be part and parcel of your romantic life this year. Travelling to distant lands and meeting unusual people will open your heart to fresh possibilities of romance.

You'll try novel and audacious things and will find yourself in a different circle of friends. Compromise will be important in making your existing relationships work. Talk about your feelings. If you are currently in a relationship you'll feel an upswing in your affection for your partner. This is a perfect opportunity to deepen your love for each other and take your relationship to a new level.

If you're not yet attached to someone, there's good news for you. Great opportunities lie in store and a spiritual or karmic connection may be experienced in 2010.

Work

Great fortune can be expected through your working life in the next twelve months. Your friends and work colleagues will want to help you achieve your goals. Even your employers will be amenable to your requests for extra money or a better position within the organisation.

If you want to start a new job or possibly begin an independent line of business, this is a great year to do it. Jupiter looks set to give you plenty of opportunities, success and a superior reputation.

Improving your luck

As long as you can keep a balanced view of things and not overdo anything, your luck will increase dramatically throughout 2010. The important thing is to remain grounded and not be too airy-fairy about your objectives. Be realistic about your talents and capabilities and don't brag about your skills or achievements. This will only invite envy from others.

Moderate your social life as well and don't drink or eat too much as this will slow your reflexes and weaken your chances for success.

You have plenty of spiritual insights this year so you should use them to their maximum. In the 1st, 8th, 15th and 24th hours of Thursdays you should use your intuition to enhance your luck, and the numbers 3, 12, 21 and 30 are also lucky for you. March and December are your lucky months but generally the whole year should go pretty smoothly for you.

4 is the year of Uranus

Overview

The electric and exciting planet of the zodiac, Uranus, and its sign of Aquarius, rule your affairs throughout 2010. Dramatic events will surprise and at the same time unnerve you in your professional and personal life. So be prepared!

You'll be able to achieve many things this year and your dreams are likely to come true, but you mustn't be distracted or scattered with your energies. You'll be breaking through your own self-limitations and this will present challenges from your family and friends. You'll want to be independent and develop your spiritual powers and nothing will stop you.

Try to maintain discipline and an orderly lifestyle so you can make the most of these special energies this year. If unexpected things do happen, it's not a bad idea to have an alternative plan so you don't lose momentum.

Love and pleasure

You want something radical, something different in your relationships this year. It's quite likely that your love life will be feeling a little less than exciting so you'll take some important steps to change that. If your partner is as progressive as you'll be this year, then your relationship is likely to improve and fulfil both of you.

In your social life you will meet some very unusual people, whom you'll feel are especially connected to you spiritually. You may want to ditch everything for the excitement and passion of a completely new relationship, but tread carefully as this may not work out exactly as you expect it to.

Work

Technology, computing and the Internet will play a larger role in your professional life this coming year.

You'll have to move ahead with the times and learn new skills if you want to achieve success.

A hectic schedule is likely, so make sure your diary is with you at all times. Try to be more efficient and don't waste time.

New friends and alliances at work will help you achieve even greater success in the coming period. Becoming a team player will be even more important in gaining satisfaction from your professional endeavours.

Improving your luck

Moving too quickly and impulsively will cause you problems on all fronts, so be a little more patient and think your decisions through more carefully. Social, romantic and professional opportunities will come to you but take a little time to investigate the ramifications of your actions.

The 1st, 8th, 15th and 20th hours of any Saturday are lucky, but love and luck are likely to cross your path when you least expect it. The numbers 4, 13, 22 and 31 are also lucky for you this year.

5 is the year of Mercury
Overview

The supreme planet of communication, Mercury, is your ruling planet throughout 2010. The number 5, which is connected to Mercury, will confer upon you success through your intellectual abilities.

Any form of writing or speaking will be improved and this will be, to a large extent, underpinning your success. Your imagination will be stimulated by this planet, with many incredible new and exciting ideas coming to mind.

Mercury and the number 5 are considered somewhat indecisive. Be firm in your attitude and don't let too many ideas or opportunities distract and confuse you. By all means get as much information as you can to help you make the right decisions.

I see you involved with money proposals, job applications, even contracts that need to be signed, so remain as clear-headed as possible.

Your business skills and clear and concise communication will be at the heart of your life in 2010.

Love and pleasure

Mercury, which rules the signs of Gemini and Virgo, will make your love life a little difficult due to its changeable nature. On the one hand you'll feel passionate and loving to your partner, yet on the other you will feel like giving it all up for the excitement of a new affair. Maintain the middle ground.

Also, try not to be too critical with your friends and family members. The influence of Virgo makes you prone to expecting much more from others than they're capable of giving. Control your sharp tongue and don't hurt people's feelings. Encouraging others is the better path, leading to greater emotional satisfaction.

Work

Speed will dominate your professional life in 2010. You'll be flitting from one subject to another and taking on far more than you can handle. You'll need to make some serious changes in your routine to handle the avalanche of work that will come your way. You'll also be travelling with your work, but not necessarily overseas.

If you're in a job you enjoy then this year will give you additional successes. If not, it may be time to move on.

Improving your luck

Communication is the key to attaining your desires in the coming twelve months. Keep focused on one idea rather than scattering your energies in all directions and your success will be speedier.

By looking after your health, sleeping well and exercising regularly, you'll build up your resilience and mental strength.

The 1st, 8th, 15th and 20th hours of Wednesday are lucky so it's best to schedule your meetings and other important social engagements during these times. The lucky numbers for Mercury are 5, 14, 23 and 32.

6 is the year of Venus

Overview

Because you're ruled by 6 this year, love is in the air! Venus, Taurus and Libra are well known for their affinity with romance, love, and even marriage. If ever you were going to meet a soulmate and feel comfortable in love, 2010 must surely be your year.

Taurus has a strong connection to money and practical affairs as well, so finances will also improve if you are diligent about work and security issues.

The important thing to keep in mind this year is that sharing love and making that important soul connection should be kept high on your agenda. This will be an enjoyable period in your life.

Love and pleasure

Romance is the key thing for you this year and your current relationships will become more fulfilling if you happen to be attached. For singles, a 6 year heralds an important meeting that eventually leads to marriage.

You'll also be interested in fashion, gifts, jewellery and all sorts of socialising. It's at one of these social engagements that you could meet the love of your life. Remain available!

Venus is one of the planets that has a tendency to overdo things, so be moderate in your eating and drinking. Try generally to maintain a modest lifestyle.

Work

You'll have a clearer insight into finances and your future security during a number 6 year. Whereas previously you may have had additional expenses and extra distractions, your mind will now be more settled and capable of longer-term planning along these lines.

With the extra cash you might see this year, decorating your home or office will give you a special sort of satisfaction.

Social affairs and professional activities will be strongly linked. Any sort of work-related functions may offer you romantic opportunities as well. On the other hand, be careful not to mix up your workplace relationships with romantic ideals. This could complicate some of your professional activities.

Improving your luck

You'll want more money and a life of leisure and ease in 2010. Keep working on your strengths and eliminate your negative personality traits to create greater luck and harmony in your life.

Moderate all your actions and don't focus exclusively on money and material objects. Feed your spiritual needs as well. By balancing your inner and outer sides you'll see that your romantic and professional lives will be enhanced more easily.

The 1st, 8th, 15th and 20th hours on Fridays will be very lucky for you and new opportunities will arise for you at those times. You can use the numbers 6, 15, 24 and 33 to increase luck in your general affairs.

7 is the year of Neptune

Overview

The last and most evolved sign of the zodiac is

Pisces, which is ruled by Neptune. The number 7 is deeply connected with this zodiac sign and governs you in 2010. Your ideals seem to be clearer and more spiritually orientated than ever before. Your desire to evolve and understand your inner self will be a double-edged sword. It depends on how organised you are as to how well you can use these spiritual and abstract concepts in your practical life.

Your past hurts and deep emotional issues will be dealt with and removed for good, if you are serious about becoming a better human being.

Spend a little more time caring for yourself rather than others, as it's likely some of your friends will drain you of energy with their own personal problems. Of course, you mustn't turn a blind eye to the needs of others, but don't ignore your own personal requirements in the process.

Love and pleasure

Meeting people with similar life views and spiritual aspirations will rekindle your faith in relationships. If you do choose to develop a new romance, make sure there is a clear understanding of the responsibilities of one to the other. Don't get swept off your feet by people who have ulterior motives.

Keep your relationships realistic and see that the most idealistic partnerships must eventually come down to Earth. Deal with the practicalities of life.

Work

This is a year of hard work, but one in which you'll

come to understand the deeper significance of your professional ideals. You may discover a whole new aspect to your career, which involves a more compassionate and self-sacrificing side to your personality.

You'll also find that your way of working will change and you'll be more focused and able to get into the spirit of whatever you do. Finding meaningful work is very likely and therefore this could be a year when money, security, creativity and spirituality overlap to bring you a great sense of personal satisfaction.

Tapping into your greater self through meditation and self-study will bring you great benefits throughout 2010.

Improving your luck

Using self-sacrifice along with discrimination will be an unusual method of improving your luck. The laws of karma state that what you give, you receive in greater measure. This is one of the principal themes for you in 2010.

The 1st, 8th, 15th and 20th hours of Tuesdays are your lucky times. The numbers 7, 16, 25 and 34 should be used to increase your lucky energies.

8 is the year of Saturn

Overview

The earthy and practical sign of Capricorn and its ruler Saturn are intimately linked to the number

8, which rules you in 2010. Your discipline and far-sightedness will help you achieve great things in the coming year. With cautious discernment, slowly but surely you will reach your goals.

It may be that due to the influence of the solitary Saturn, your best work and achievement will be behind closed doors away from the limelight. You mustn't fear this as you'll discover many new things about yourself. You'll learn just how strong you really are.

Love and pleasure

Work will overshadow your personal affairs in 2010, but you mustn't let this erode the personal relationships you have. Becoming a workaholic brings great material successes but will also cause you to become too insular and aloof. Your family members won't take too kindly to you working 100-hour weeks.

Responsibility is one of the key words for this number and you will therefore find yourself in a position of authority that leaves very little time for fun. Try to make the time to enjoy the company of friends and family and by all means schedule time off on the weekends as it will give you the peace of mind you're looking for.

Because of your responsible attitude it will be very hard for you not to assume a greater role in your workplace and this indicates longer working hours with the likelihood of a promotion with equally good remuneration.

Work

Money is high on your agenda in 2010. Number 8 is a good money number according to the Chinese and this year is at last likely to bring you the fruits of your hard labour. You are cautious and resourceful in all your dealings and will not waste your hard-earned savings. You will also be very conscious of using your time wisely.

You will be given more responsibilities and you're likely to take them on, if only to prove to yourself that you can handle whatever life dishes up.

Expect a promotion in which you'll play a leading role in your work. Your diligence and hard work will pay off, literally, in a bigger salary and more respect from others.

Improving your luck

Caution is one of the key characteristics of the number 8 and is linked to Capricorn. But being overly cautious could cause you to miss valuable opportunities. If an offer is put to you, try to think outside the square and balance it with your naturally cautious nature.

Be gentle and kind to yourself. By loving yourself, others will naturally love you, too. The 1st, 8th, 15th and 20th hours of Saturdays are exceptionally lucky for you, as are the numbers 1, 8, 17, 26 and 35.

9 is the year of Mars

Overview

You are now entering the final year of a nine-year cycle dominated by the planet Mars and the sign of Aries. You'll be completing many things and are determined to be successful after several years of intense work.

Some of your relationships may now have reached their use-by date and even personal affairs may need to be released. Don't let arguments and disagreements get in the road of friendly resolution in these areas of your life.

Mars is a challenging planet, and this year, although you will be very active and productive, you may find others trying to obstruct the achievement of your goals. As a result you may react strongly to them, thereby creating disharmony in your workplace. Don't be so impulsive or reckless, and generally slow things down. The slower, steadier approach has greater merit this year.

Love and pleasure

If you become too bossy and pushy with friends this year you will just end up pushing them out of your life. It's a year to end certain friendships but by the same token it could be the perfect time to remove conflicts and thereby bolster your love affairs in 2010.

If you're feeling a little irritable and angry with those you love, try getting rid of these negative feelings through some intense, rigorous sports and physical activity. This will definitely relieve tension and improve your personal life.

Work

Because you're healthy and able to work at a more intense pace you'll achieve an incredible amount in the coming year. Overwork could become a problem if you're not careful.

Because the number 9 and Mars are infused with leadership energy, you'll be asked to take the reins of the job and steer your company or group in a certain direction. This will bring with it added responsibility but also a greater sense of purpose for you.

Improving your luck

Because of the hot and restless energy of the number 9, it is important to create more mental peace in your life this year. Lower the temperature, so to speak, and decompress your relationships rather than becoming aggravated. Try to talk with your work partners and loved ones rather than telling them what to do. This will generally pick up your health and your relationships.

The 1st, 8th, 15th and 20th hours of Tuesdays are the luckiest for you this year and, if you're involved in any disputes or need to attend to health issues, these times are also very good to get the best results. Your lucky numbers are 9, 18, 27 and 36

2010:
Your Daily Planner

The man of wisdom is never of two minds;
the man of benevolence never worries; the man of
courage is never afraid

—Confucius

According to astrology, the success of any venture or activity is dependent upon the planetary positions at the time you commence that activity. Electional astrology helps you select the most appropriate times for many of your day-to-day endeavours. These dates are applicable to each and every zodiac sign and can be used freely by one and all, even if your star sign doesn't fall under the one mentioned in this book. Please note that the daily planner is a universal system applicable equally to all *twelve* star signs. Anyone and everyone can use this planner irrespective of their birth sign.

Ancient astrologers understood the planetary patterns and how they impacted on each of us. This allowed them to suggest the best possible times to start various important activities. For example, many farmers still use this approach today: they understand the phases of the Moon, and attest to the fact that planting seeds on certain lunar days produces a far better crop than does planting on other days.

In the following section, many facets of daily life are considered. Using the lunar cycle and the combined strength of other planets allows us to work out the best times to do them. This is your personal almanac, which can be used in conjunction with any star sign to help optimise the results.

First, select the activity you are interested in, and then quickly scan the year for the best months to start it. When you have selected the month, you can finetune your timing by finding the best specific dates. You can then be sure that the planetary energies will be in sync with you, offering you the best possible outcome.

Coupled with what you know about your monthly and weekly trends, the daily planner is an effective tool to help you capitalise on opportunities that come your way this year.

Good luck, and may the planets bless you with great success, fortune and happiness in 2010!

Getting started in 2010

How many times have you made a new year's resolution to begin a diet or be a better person in your relationships? And, how many times has it not worked out? Well, part of the reason may be that you started out at the wrong time, because how successful you are is strongly influenced by the position of the Moon and the planets when you begin a particular activity. You will be more successful with the following endeavours if you start them on the days indicated.

Relationships

We all feel more empowered on some days than on others. This is because the planets have some power over us—their movement and their relationships to each other determine the ebb and flow of our energies. And, our levels of self-confidence and sense of romantic magnetism play an important part in the way we behave in relationships.

Your daily planner tells you the ideal dates for meeting new friends, initiating a love affair, spending time with family and loved ones—it even tells you the most appropriate times for sexual encounters.

You'll be surprised at how much more impact you will make in your relationships when you tune yourself in to the planetary energies on these special dates.

Falling in love/restoring love

During these times you could expect favourable energies to meet your soulmate or, if you've had difficulty in a relationship, to approach the one you love to rekindle both your and their emotional responses:

January	18, 20, 23, 24
February	15, 16, 20, 24
March	29
April	16
May	14, 17, 18, 19, 20, 23
June	14, 15, 16, 20, 21
July	12
August	10, 13, 14
September	9, 21, 22
October	8, 18, 19, 20
November	14, 15, 16, 19, 20, 21
December	13, 17, 18

Special times with friends and family

Socialising, partying and having a good time with those whose company you enjoy is highly favourable under the following dates. They are excellent to spend time with family and loved ones in a domestic environment:

January	6, 26, 27
February	12, 13, 14, 15, 16, 20, 24
March	11, 21, 22, 29, 30, 31
April	8
May	15, 16, 17, 18, 19, 20, 23, 24
June	1, 2, 3, 11, 12, 14, 15, 16, 20, 21, 29, 30
July	8, 9, 12, 17, 18, 26, 27
August	5, 6, 9, 10, 13, 14, 22, 23, 24
September	1, 2, 5, 9, 10, 18, 19, 20, 30
October	3, 19, 20, 25, 26, 30, 31
November	3, 4, 14, 15, 16, 22, 26, 27
December	2, 9, 10, 11, 19, 20, 24, 25

Healing or resuming relationships

If you're trying to get back together with the one you love or need a heart-to-heart or deep-and-meaningful discussion with someone, you can try the following dates to do so:

January	12, 13, 14, 15, 21, 22, 23, 24, 25
February	6
March	6, 31
April	2, 7, 8, 12, 16, 19, 23, 24, 25, 26

May	10, 11, 12, 13, 14, 15, 16, 17, 18, 19, 20, 21,22, 23, 24, 25, 26, 27, 28, 30
June	3, 8, 9, 10, 11, 12, 13, 14, 15, 16, 17, 21, 22, 23, 25, 26, 27, 28, 29, 30
July	1, 2, 3, 4, 5, 10, 11, 12, 13, 15, 16, 17, 18, 19, 20, 21, 22, 23, 28, 29, 30
August	1, 2, 3, 4, 5, 6, 9, 10, 13, 14, 15, 16, 20, 23, 25, 26, 27
September	2, 5, 9, 10, 13, 17, 18, 19, 20
October	1, 2, 3, 6, 12, 13, 14, 15, 20, 22, 23, 24, 25, 26, 27, 28, 29, 30, 31
November	3, 4, 5, 6, 7, 8, 9, 21, 27, 28, 29, 30
December	2, 3, 4, 6, 12, 13, 14, 17, 18, 19, 20, 21, 23, 24, 25

Sexual encounters

Physical and sexual energies are well favoured on the following dates. The energies of the planets enhance your moments of intimacy during these times:

January	1, 6, 7, 21, 22
February	6, 12, 13, 14, 20, 24
March	14, 15, 17, 18, 19, 30, 31
April	23, 24, 25, 26
May	9, 12, 14, 17, 18, 19, 20
June	3, 8, 9, 10, 11, 14, 15, 16, 20, 21, 29, 30
July	8, 9, 10, 11, 12
August	6, 10, 13, 14, 22, 23, 24

September   3, 4, 5, 6, 9, 10, 18, 19, 20, 21, 22, 30
October   1, 2, 3, 7, 8, 18, 19, 20, 23, 24, 28, 29, 30, 31
November   3, 4, 14, 15, 16, 19, 24, 25, 26, 27
December   2, 10, 11, 12, 13, 15, 16, 17, 19, 20, 22, 23,
             24, 25

Health and wellbeing

Your aura and life force are susceptible to the movements of the planets—in particular, they respond to the phases of the Moon.

The following dates are the most appropriate times to begin a diet, have cosmetic surgery, or seek medical advice. They also indicate the best times to help others.

Feeling of wellbeing

Your physical as well as your mental alertness should be strong on these following dates. You can plan your activities and expect a good response from others:

January   2, 3, 4, 5, 6, 7, 11, 12, 13, 14, 16, 17, 18,
            21, 22, 23, 24, 30, 31
February   1, 2, 7, 8, 15, 16, 17, 18, 19, 20, 21, 22, 23,
            24, 25, 26, 27, 28
March   16, 17, 18, 19, 20, 22, 23, 24, 25, 26, 27,
            28, 29
April   7, 13, 14, 16, 28
May   2, 11, 14, 25, 26
June   8, 22, 23, 26, 27, 28, 29, 30

July	4, 5, 8, 9, 12, 13, 14, 15, 16, 19, 20, 23, 24, 25
August	5, 6, 9, 10, 11, 12, 13, 15, 16, 20, 21
September	9, 10, 11, 12, 13, 16, 17, 21, 22, 24, 25, 28, 29, 30
October	3, 4, 5, 6, 7, 8, 9, 10, 13, 14, 15, 22
November	4, 5, 6, 10, 11, 19, 20, 21
December	7, 8, 17, 18, 28, 29

Healing and medicine

These times are good for approaching others who have expertise when you need some deeper understanding. They are also favourable for any sort of healing or medication and making appointments with doctors or psychologists. Planning surgery around these dates should bring good results.

Often giving up our time and energy to assist others doesn't necessarily result in the expected outcome. However, by lending a helping hand to a friend on the following dates, the results should be favourable:

January	1, 2, 3, 4, 6, 7, 8, 9, 11, 12, 13, 14, 15, 16, 17, 18, 19, 20, 21, 22, 23, 24, 26, 27, 28, 29, 30, 31
February	1, 5, 6, 9, 11, 12, 13, 14, 15, 16, 19
March	1, 2, 3, 4, 5, 8, 9, 10, 11, 12, 18, 19, 24, 25, 29
April	1, 3, 4, 5, 22, 26
May	4, 5

June	1, 2, 3, 9, 10, 17, 18, 22, 23, 24, 25, 29, 30
July	6, 7, 15, 16, 17, 18, 19, 21, 22, 23, 24, 25, 26
August	2, 3, 4, 11, 12, 17, 18, 19, 20, 21, 30, 31
September	6, 7, 8, 10, 11, 12, 13, 14, 15, 16, 17, 18, 26, 27, 28, 29
October	5, 7, 8, 9, 10, 11, 12, 13, 14, 15, 16, 17, 18, 19, 20, 21, 22, 23, 24, 25, 26, 28, 29, 30, 31
November	1, 2, 3, 5, 7, 8, 10, 11, 14, 15, 17, 18, 19, 22, 23
December	4, 5, 7, 8, 9, 10, 12, 13, 14, 16, 23, 24, 25, 26, 28, 29, 30, 31

Money

Money is an important part of life, and involves many decisions—decisions about borrowing, investing, spending. The ideal times for transactions are very much influenced by the planets, and whether your investment or nest egg grows or doesn't grow can often be linked to timing. Making your decisions on the following dates could give you a whole new perspective on your financial future.

Managing wealth and money

To build your nest egg it's a good time to open your bank account or invest money on the following dates:

January	1, 6, 7, 13, 14, 15, 18, 21, 22, 28, 29
February	3, 4, 9, 10, 11, 12, 13, 14, 15, 17, 18, 24, 25
March	2, 3, 9, 10, 16, 17, 18, 23, 24, 29, 30, 31

April	5, 6, 7, 13, 14, 19, 20, 21, 26, 27,
May	2, 3, 4, 10, 11, 17, 18, 23, 24, 30, 31
June	6, 7, 8, 13, 14, 19, 20, 21, 26, 27, 28
July	4, 5, 10, 11, 12, 17, 18, 23, 24, 25, 31
August	1, 7, 8, 13, 14, 20, 21, 27, 28, 29
September	3, 4, 9, 10, 16, 17, 23, 24, 25
October	1, 2, 7, 8, 13, 14, 15, 21, 22, 28, 29
November	3, 4, 10, 11, 17, 18, 24, 25
December	1, 2, 7, 8, 14, 15, 16, 21, 22, 23, 24, 29

Spending

It's always fun to spend but the following dates are more in tune with this activity and are likely to give you better results:

January	3, 4, 5, 6, 7, 8, 9, 10, 11, 12, 13, 14
February	3, 4, 5, 10, 19
March	8, 10, 11, 13, 14, 19
April	7, 8, 11, 12, 22
May	6, 7, 8, 9, 10, 11, 12, 13, 17, 18, 19, 20, 21, 22, 23, 24, 25, 26, 27, 28
June	1, 11, 12, 14, 16, 17, 19, 23, 25, 26, 27, 28, 29, 30
July	6, 7, 8, 23, 24, 25, 26, 27, 28, 29, 31
August	1, 2, 3, 4, 5, 15, 16, 17, 18, 19, 30, 31
September	1, 2, 3, 4, 17, 18, 19, 20, 21, 22, 23, 27, 28, 29, 30
October	4, 7, 12, 13, 14, 15, 16, 17, 18, 19, 27, 28

November	2, 3, 4, 25, 26, 27, 28
December	11, 22, 23

Selling

If you're thinking of selling something, whether it is small or large, consider the following dates as ideal times to do so:

January	18
February	12, 13, 14, 15
March	5, 6, 9, 14, 15, 16, 17, 18, 19, 21
April	1, 3, 4, 5, 22, 26
May	7, 12, 21, 29
June	3, 8, 9, 10, 11, 12, 13, 17, 24, 25, 26, 27, 28, 30
July	1, 2, 7, 9, 10, 11, 25, 27, 28, 29, 30, 31
August	1, 2, 3, 4, 5, 6, 7, 8, 9, 10, 13, 20, 23, 28
September	2, 9, 10, 11, 12, 13, 14, 15, 16, 17, 18, 19, 20, 21, 22, 23, 24, 26, 30
October	1, 2, 3, 4, 6, 7, 10, 11, 17, 18, 19, 20, 21, 22, 23, 24, 25, 27, 29
November	3, 4, 5, 6, 7, 11, 14, 15, 16, 17, 18, 19, 21, 23, 24, 25, 26, 27, 28, 29, 30
December	1, 2, 3, 4, 5, 6, 7, 8, 9, 10, 11, 12, 13, 14, 15, 16, 17, 18, 19, 20, 21, 22

Borrowing

Few of us like to borrow money, but if you must, taking out a loan on the following dates will be positive:

January	12, 30
February	7, 12, 13
March	6, 7, 8, 11
April	3, 4, 8
May	9, 28, 29
June	1, 2, 3, 4, 5, 29, 30
July	1, 2, 3, 26, 27, 28, 29, 30
August	9, 25, 26
September	5, 6
October	3, 30
November	26, 27
December	3, 4, 21, 22, 23, 30, 31

Work and education

Your career is important, and continual improvement of your skills is therefore also crucial professionally, mentally and socially. The dates below will help you find out the most appropriate times to improve your professional talents and commence new work or education associated with your work.

You may need to decide when to start learning a new skill, when to ask for a promotion, and even when to make an important career change. Here are the days when your mental and educational power is strong.

Learning new skills

Educational pursuits are lucky and bring good results on the following dates:

January	15, 16, 17, 18, 19, 20, 21, 22, 25, 26, 27
February	14, 15, 16, 17, 18, 19, 22, 23, 28
March	16, 17, 18, 21, 22, 27, 28
April	17, 18, 24, 25
May	15, 16, 21, 22
June	12, 17, 18, 24, 25
July	15, 16, 21, 22, 23, 24, 25
August	11, 12, 17, 18, 19
September	8, 13, 15, 20, 21, 22
October	11, 12
November	7, 8, 9
December	6, 19, 20

Changing career path or profession

If you're feeling stuck and need to move into a new professional activity, changing jobs could be done at these times:

January	6, 7, 15, 16, 17, 23, 24
February	12, 13, 14, 19, 20, 21
March	19, 20, 27, 28
April	15, 16, 24, 25
May	14, 21, 22
June	17, 18, 19, 20, 21
July	8, 9, 15, 16, 23, 24, 25

August	5, 6, 11, 12, 20, 21, 22, 23
September	1, 2, 8, 13, 14, 15, 17
October	8, 13, 14, 15, 16, 17
November	3, 4, 10, 11, 19, 20, 21
December	1, 2, 3, 7, 8, 17, 18, 28, 29

Promotion, professional focus and hard work

To increase your mental focus and achieve good results from the work you do; promotions are also likely on these dates:

January	4, 5, 6, 11, 12, 13, 14, 15, 16, 17, 18, 19, 21
February	6
March	16, 17, 18, 19, 20, 21, 23, 24, 25, 26, 27, 28, 29
April	8, 28, 29
May	12, 21
June	25, 26, 27, 28
July	4, 5, 8, 9, 12, 13, 14, 15, 16, 17, 18, 19, 20, 21, 22, 23, 24, 25, 26, 27
August	5, 6, 10, 11, 12, 13, 14, 15, 16, 17, 18, 19, 20, 21, 22, 23, 24
September	13, 14, 15
October	10, 11, 12, 13, 14, 15, 17, 18, 19, 20, 22, 23, 24, 30, 31
November	2, 4, 5, 6, 7, 8, 9, 23, 24, 25, 26, 27, 28, 29, 30
December	2, 3, 4, 11, 12, 13, 14, 15, 16, 18, 19, 20, 21, 23, 24, 25

Travel

Setting out on a holiday or adventurous journey is exciting. Here are the most favourable times for doing this. Travel on the following dates is likely to give you a sense of fulfilment:

January	15
February	15, 16, 18, 19, 20, 21
March	16, 17, 18, 21, 22, 23
April	19, 24, 25, 26, 27
May	16, 17, 18, 21, 22
June	17, 18, 19, 20, 21, 24, 25
July	21, 22, 23, 24, 25
August	19
September	9, 21, 22
October	18, 19, 20, 21, 22
November	7, 16, 17, 18
December	6, 14, 16, 19, 20

Beauty and grooming

Believe it or not, cutting your hair or nails has a powerful effect on your body's electromagnetic energy. If you cut your hair or nails at the wrong time of the month, you can reduce your level of vitality significantly. Use these dates to ensure you optimise your energy levels by staying in tune with the stars.

Hair and nails

January	1, 2, 3, 4, 5, 6, 7, 8, 11, 12, 13, 14, 15, 18, 19, 20, 21, 22, 25, 26, 27
February	3, 4, 5, 7, 8, 15, 16, 17, 18, 19, 22, 23, 24, 25
March	2, 3, 4, 6, 7, 8, 14, 15, 21, 22
April	1, 2, 3, 4, 5, 10, 11, 12, 17, 18, 19, 20, 21, 22, 23, 28, 29, 30
May	1, 2, 3, 4, 5, 7, 8, 9, 10, 11, 12, 13, 15, 16, 17, 18, 25, 26 27, 28, 29, 30
June	4, 5, 11, 12, 14, 15, 16, 24, 25
July	1, 2, 3, 8, 9, 12, 13, 14, 21, 22, 28, 29, 30
August	1, 2, 5, 6, 17, 18, 19, 25, 26
September	1, 2, 6, 7, 14, 15, 21, 22, 23, 24, 28, 29, 30
October	3, 4, 11, 12, 18, 19, 20, 25, 26, 27, 28, 29, 30
November	7, 8, 9, 14, 15, 16, 22, 23, 24, 25, 26, 27
December	5, 6, 12, 13, 19, 20, 21, 22, 23, 24, 25

Therapies, massage and self-pampering

January	6, 7, 13, 14, 15, 18, 19, 20, 21
February	2, 3, 9, 11, 14
March	1, 9, 14, 16, 17, 20, 23, 29
April	4, 5, 6, 10, 11, 12, 13, 17, 25, 26
May	2, 3, 7, 8, 9, 10, 11, 14, 15, 16, 17, 22, 23, 24, 31
June	3, 5, 12, 18, 19, 26, 27
July	4, 7, 8, 9, 10, 16, 23, 28, 29, 30, 31
August	3, 4, 5, 6, 7, 13, 20, 21, 24, 25, 26, 27, 28, 31
September	2, 17, 21, 28, 29

October	13, 14, 15, 18, 19, 21, 25, 26, 27, 28
November	2, 3, 9, 11, 14, 15, 16, 17, 21, 24, 29
December	7, 12, 13, 14, 15, 18, 19, 20, 22, 26, 27, 28, 29

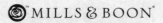

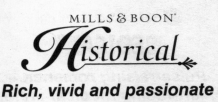
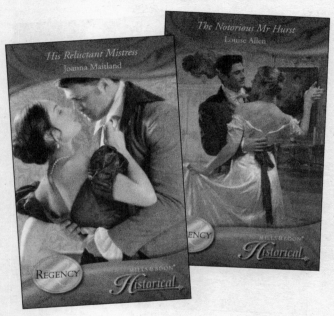

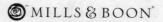

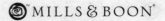

millsandboon.co.uk Community

Join Us!

The Community is the perfect place to meet and chat to kindred spirits who love books and reading as much as you do, but it's also the place to:

- ■ Get the inside scoop from authors about their latest books
- ■ Learn how to write a romance book with advice from our editors
- ■ Help us to continue publishing the best in women's fiction
- ■ Share your thoughts on the books we publish
- ■ Befriend other users

Forums: Interact with each other as well as authors, editors and a whole host of other users worldwide.

Blogs: Every registered community member has their own blog to tell the world what they're up to and what's on their mind.

Book Challenge: We're aiming to read 5,000 books and have joined forces with The Reading Agency in our inaugural Book Challenge.

Profile Page: Showcase yourself and keep a record of your recent community activity.

Social Networking: We've added buttons at the end of every post to share via digg, Facebook, Google, Yahoo, technorati and de.licio.us.

www.millsandboon.co.uk

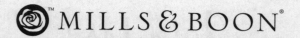